DATE DUE

DE			
NO 17 '01			
OC			
JE 7 '06			

DEMCO 38-296

THE STATE OF TERROR

SUNY Series in Deviance and Social Control

Ronald A. Farrell, Editor

THE STATE OF TERROR

ANNAMARIE OLIVERIO

FOREWORD BY ANDRE GUNDER FRANK

AFTERWORD BY PAT LAUDERDALE

STATE UNIVERSITY OF NEW YORK PRESS

Published by
State University of New York Press, Albany

For information, address State University of New York Press,
State University Plaza, Albany, N.Y. 12246

Production by M. R. Mulholland
Marketing by Nancy Farrell

Library of Congress Cataloging-in-Publication Data

Oliverio, Annamarie, 1961–
    The state of terror / Annamarie Oliverio.
       p.   cm. — (SUNY series in deviance and social control)
    Includes bibliographical references (p.   ) and index.
    ISBN 0-7914-3707-8 (alk. paper). — ISBN 0-7914-3708-6 (pb. : alk.
paper)
    1. Terrorism. 2. International relations. 3. Terrorism in mass
media—United States. 4. Terrorism in mass media—Italy. 5. Mass
media—Political aspects. 6. Terrorism—Case studies. 7. Achille
Lauro Hijacking Incident, 1985. 8. TWA Flight 847 Hijacking
Incident, 1985. I. Title. II. Series.
HV6431.O55 1998
303.6'25—dc21   97-17274
                                                                                            CIP

To
Emma, Fausto, Almeta, T.E.,
and all the unmarked victims of terrorism

CONTENTS

FOREWORD

Big brother is brainwashing you—with "terrorist" doubles-peak, according to Oliverio. She, like I, laments and rejects terrorism, not to mention violence, be it the *Achille Lauro* affair and the TWA hijacking that she analyzes in detail or the bomb in Oklahoma City and those placed by the Unabomber, which she mentions. However, the author's focus and therefore also my own here is not only on the acts of terrorism by terrorists, but on their portrayal and manipulation by others, and particularly on the media's construction of "terrorism" for statist purposes. By comparing Italian and American state and media presentations of the *Achille Lauro*/TWA cases, Oliverio is able to demonstrate how "terrorism" is presented differently in accord with differing state interests in these two events. Oliverio is intent on distinguishing between "the rhetoric of terror and the terror of rhetoric." Thus, she focuses "on the practical production of social and political constructions of terrorism." In Oliverio's book, "terrorism" is not so much an act as a *definition* of it. So, what really makes "terrorism" is the power to *define* it. According to Oliverio, "terrorism is a construct that is best understood as a relative rhetoric of the state, intrinsic to statecraft"—and so is what is not to be called "terrorism."

Oliverio intentionally and admittedly departs from the "mainstream" treatment of "terrorism" and instead examines it "from a framework similar to witch hunts, or the scapegoating of the counterculture." That is, she devotes most of her attention to analyzing and critiquing how the concept of "terrorism" is—and is not—used for statist purposes by the powers that be, and especially by the American state. These purposes are, she argues, essentially to "stage manage" crises and social unrest by scapegoating and/or denial or diversion through brainwashing, in this case through the use of charges of "terrorism." She quotes a former Attorney General of the United States, Ramsey Clark:

"The things that create the greatest terror in life by far are rarely called 'terrorism' . . . and the things we call terrorism, horrible in human terms as they are, are overwhelmingly the acts of powerless people." By extension, on the other hand, those who have power, including the power *to define*, never engage in "terrorism"—by their own definition!

Oliverio reserves her severest critiques for those who specialize in making these *definitions* of "terrorism" largely on behalf of the state. Though these people and institutions may take their guidelines from their own states, they may be found especially in academia and the media, where they have developed "terrorism into a field of study in its own right with its own experts specializing in knowing and identifying terror." Their concepts and analyses are outmoded, and they parade their own ideology and especially American state interests as ostensible scientific discourse about alleged objective truth. They construct "profiles of terrorists" as consciousless criminals, and they point fingers at whole societies and their political leaders: "Terrorism, for example, is often associated with distant, foreign regimes depicted as completely different from North America. The Pol Pot regime in Kampuchea, and those of Amin in Uganda, Allende in Chile, Castro in Cuba, Khomeini in Iran, Quadhafi in Libya, Noriega in Panama, or Hussein in Iraq, to name a few, are cited as typically terrorist societies." As a result, all sorts of acts of violence are immediately and routinely blamed on Palestinian and other Middle Eastern scapegoats. Oliverio cites some cases in the early 1990s and notes that the American press immediately blamed the bombing of the Oklahoma City Federal Building on "Arabs"; many were harangued by their neighbors, and the American authorities had a Palestinian arrested in London before they turned their attention to real home grown terrorists.

By appealing to the metaphor of the theater, Oliverio is able to show how Americans and Italians perceived, reported, and handled the *Achille Lauro* incident and TWA hijacking differently, as in an Italian Pirandello play or the Japanese Rashomon movie. In America, the state and the media perceived, presented, and condemned both as acts of "terrorism" pure and simple. Oliverio argues that it was in the U.S. state interest to do so, and that the media enthusiastically obliged in portraying unadulterated villainy and evil. In Italy, cultural perceptions of the same events were different and much more sensitive to the Palestinian actors. The Italian media, executive branch, and judicial system had much more understanding for and compassion with the events. The judicial system gave due consideration to the sociopolitical background and motives, as well as to the psychology, of the Palestinian actors. Some Italians accused the American superpower of exerting "terrorist" pressure against the Italian client state to do the American bidding to use armed intervention where and when, to Italian eyes, it was not warranted.

The geopolitical interests of the two states were in conflict. Each state used the same events to serve its own political power or power politics interests and in so doing characterized them differently. Oliverio demonstrates convincingly how not so much the events in themselves, but their interested presentations by the American and Italian states and media determined whether they were "terrorism" or not. For perceptions tend to differ on many issues in a hegemonic state, where people are inclined to equate their views with universalism, form perceptions about the same issues in subaltern, not to mention dependent states, where conflicts of interest are much more apparent. Such differences of perspective on various issues of the "civilizing mission" certainly marked the colonialist and imperialist eras. So it should not be too surprising to find analogous differences of opinion also today about various issues, including "terrorism."

Another incident offers further vivid illustrations of how states' interests differently guide their own and their media's perception of and reaction to "terrorism." A decade ago, American planes bombed civilians in Libya "in retaliation" for Libya's alleged sponsorship of a terrorist attack in Berlin. Mrs. Thatcher's Britain gave permission for (and its press took pride in) America's use of British air bases to depart on their bombing mission to Libya. However, the planes had to fly the long way around the Atlantic (and one was lost as a result) because the

allied governments of France, Spain, and Italy remained uncon-
vinced and refused to allow the American war planes into their
airspace. The American military attack on civilians, in which,
among others, a child of Quadhafi died, was defined by the
President of the United States, the Prime Minister of the United
Kingdom, their governments, and their media as no more than
a justified response to the alleged terrorism of others. Later evidence published by the American press showed that the responsibility for the events in Berlin did not lie with Libya at all, but
elsewhere. Different states had interpreted and used "terrorism"
quite differently in the service of their own interests, which had
precious little to do with events in Berlin or their alleged insti-
gation by Libya.

Beyond supporting her arguments by citing Edmund
Burke and Alexis de Tocqueville, Oliverio also quotes Justice of
the Supreme Court Louis Brandeis and the American historian
Henry Steele Commanger with regard to terrorism by the state
itself. The latter wrote that "Americans, too, must confess their
own history of terrorism against those they feared or hated or
regarded as 'lesser breeds,'" with examples ranging from the
extermination of Indians at home to the burning down of Mylai
in Vietnam. Justice Brandeis observed that "if government
becomes a lawbreaker it breeds contempt for the law." Yet, Oliverio notes, "terrorism" has been so redefined (or refined?) as to
exclude saturation bombing of civilians in Europe and Asia, and
indeed atomic bombing, or "precision" bombing in Iraq. She
cites Commanger as writing that this type of action is "the formal rationalization—we might almost say legitimization—of
terrorism," but without calling it that!

Therein, Oliverio is at pains to show that state interests and
ideological construction of what is politically convenient to term
and condemn as "terrorism" also automatically exclude what is
convenient to reject or even criticize. She argues that there is
indeed still much state terrorism or state-sponsored/supported
terrorism. Of course, that charge is also made by many in the
West, and especially in America, when reference is to an Islamic
state that is not an ally, like Saudi Arabia. So what Quadhafi and
Hussein do is terrorism; but it is not so, as Oliverio observes, to

use "smart bombs"—also used to "precision" bomb power plants used for waterworks and sewage systems in Iraq. Nor is it "terrorism" to starve civilians through a continuing embargo on Iraq that the American oil companies now reveal increases the price of oil!

Definitions and charges of "terrorism" also change in accord with "reasons of state": Noriega was first an American agent photographed with George Bush, who then branded Noriega a "terrorist." Therefore, it was not "terrorism" for President Bush to invade Panama and bomb/burn low-income housing in Panama City in order to bring Noriega to "justice" in the United States. The "terrorist" label has also never been applied to any actions undertaken, sponsored, or condoned by the United States or its agencies like the CIA, not even to its notorious "dirty tricks" and collaboration with military dictatorships around the world, which were condemned and forbidden by the United States Congress. Nor was any of the Iran-Contra affair, also denounced by the United States Congress, termed "terrorist." Neither was the mining of a harbor in Nicaragua, which was declared a gross violation of international law by the International Court of Justice in the Hague, with the result that the United States denied the Court's jurisdiction!

Similarly, it would be politically taboo, indeed immediately derided as "antisemitism," to apply the "terrorist" term to anything that the Israeli state has routinely practiced since 1967 in the territories it occupied, or in those that it did not occupy but instead bombed, as in Lebanon on several occasions, including again during the two weeks prior to this writing. And what exempts the British state from charges of routine state—and army of occupation—terrorism for twenty-five years in Northern Ireland and in its notorious H block prisons? And speaking of prisons, Oliverio asks why the United States is also exempt from charges of "terrorism" when more of its young African American males are locked away in prison and on parole than in "normal" society, not to mention in school? And, asks Oliverio, what about the ten thousand people, also predominantly African Americans, who are killed every year in the United

States by handguns? She observes that "practices such as spousal or child abuse, racism, gang violence, environmental destruction, poverty, or even medical malpractice and abuse, to name a few, are not recognized as terrorism." Neither are, she observes, the violence of poverty, disease, exploitation, or oppression in the Third World, nor the economic policies imposed by the International Monetary Fund, which have aggravated the same. Why not?

Why not, indeed?! The brunt of Oliverio's analysis and message goes far beyond "terrorism" narrowly defined, or even of the sociopolitical construction of "terrorism." Her appeal is not really for more comprehension for the poor and weak, for some of whom acts of individual terror may be the desperate response or the last affordable resistance to oppression. Oliverio's powerful appeal is to comprehend that it is the state, including especially the academy and the media, who serve their own interests by labelling, denouncing, and persecuting the powerless as the sources of "terrorism." Concomitantly, Oliverio also appeals to our comprehension of how the same interested parties use this same power to shape our perceptions in their (largely successful) attempt to protect themselves from the terrorist label and other critiques and to exempt their policies from reform. For, she argues, their own policies help to create and support the social/political/economic conditions at home and abroad, which benefit the rich and powerful at the cost of the poor and weak among (some of) whom they generate the very responses, defenses, and counterattacks that are then condemned as "terrorism."

Oliverio's topic, her title notwithstanding therefore, is not just terrorism, the state, or the latter's definitions of the former. Her concern and the implications of her study encompass the entire societal and indeed world-wide structure of power and power of structure. For she illuminates how these maintain and propagate themselves, not the least by how they define "deviance" from the structure of inequality and the injustice of power. For these are themselves set up and defined as the norm by these same powers who then combat those deviants who seek to escape from or combat the same. Thus, one important way that the status quo is maintained is by brainwashing people at home and abroad to accept as normal what should ideally be abnormal and to reject all deviance therefrom as itself abnormal "terrorism."

Andre Gunder Frank

PREFACE

The State of Terror is a metaphor for the symbiotic relationship between the state and terrorism. When terrorism is juxtaposed with the state the research implications are not only complex, but deeply political. To begin with, *The State of Terror* is a
comparative analysis of what is considered to be one of the most
devastating social problems of the contemporary world. Second,
it is a study of the social construction of deviants, in this case,
defined as terrorists. Third, it examines hegemony and its production by the state in a mass-mediated culture and explicates
the integrative, yet competitive practices of power, knowledge,
and politics and the production of social change. Fourth, this
book is about discourse and text: the power of words in constructing and interpreting definitions of reality or, conversely,
obfuscating them. In general, this book explores two cultures,
the United States and Italy, under a perceived threat of siege
defined as "terrorism" and how each engages and competes
between culturally specific and internationally informed practices of power in resolving the seemingly impervious problem
called terrorism. The United States is currently a site of discursive struggle regarding terrorism. In the seventies, Italy was a
site of discursive struggle regarding terrorism, while today such
terrorism is no longer perceived as a threat to the Italian state.
Examining two climactic terrorist events such as the *Achille
Lauro* affair and TWA hijacking, at the same moment in time, yet
at different moments of social construction (or deconstruction)
may provide important insights into terrorism itself and its
effective demise.

The book is organized into three main parts, utilizing the
dominant theater metaphor emerging from both sites of struggle. Thus, the first part sets the stage and writes the script. The
second part is a systematic examination of constructed mean-

ings surrounding the *Achille Lauro*/TWA dramas in each site of discursive struggle. The third part, the epilogue, provides a disquieted resolution and a path for future research.

Acknowledgments

In the process of writing of this book, a number of people provided me with their intellectual insights, support and inspiration. Richard Ashley was central to its conception. I thank him for his unrestrictive, creative guidance. I thank Henry Walker, Raymond Corrado, Nachman Ben-Yehuda, and Morris Zelditch Jr. for their very thoughtful and valuable comments on the entire manuscript. The careful examination and suggestions of the anonymous reviewers also made a number of improvements possible. Earlier drafts of the book were read by Piero Baldini, Ron Farrell, Pat McGowan, Andrew Kirby, Vron Ware, and Gabriel Kuhn who provided me with critical insights and enthusiasm about the project. Piero Baldini was also very helpful at double-checking my translations of Italian texts. David Goldberg and Ugo Colella provided important insights in the Afterword. I also appreciate the critiques of Nancy Howell and others for their thoughtful comments on the Foreword. I am honored for the chance to appreciate the eloquence of Andre Gunder Frank, whose experience and intellectual wisdom are reflected in his provocative contribution to this work.

I also thank my parents, Emma and Fausto, and my sisters, Gilda and Aurora, who from across the continent and the Atlantic have provided me with an endless supply of information, ideas, and spiritual support. My young daughters, Daniela and Patricia, have also been significantly patient and without their patience this work might not have been possible, with a little additional help from Berthis Anderson. The technical support of the Department of Sociology at Stanford University, the Institute for Political Science at the University of Innsbruck, Austria, and the Department of Social and Behavioral Sciences at Arizona State University West are greatly appreciated. The efforts of Christine Worden were essential for the publication of this book, along with the work of Jennie R. Doling, Katy

Leonard, Judy Spevak, Zina Lawrence, Megeen Mulholland, Nancy Farrell and others from the SUNY Press staff.

I am particularly grateful for the critiques, questions, challenges, and contribution(s) of Pat Lauderdale. His undying passion and persistence in supporting my work have been invaluable.

PART I

INTRODUCTION

1

Prologue

A recent report on terrorism by the U.S. State Department indicated that twenty-five citizens were killed by terrorist acts in 1986. The report concluded that if there is to be peace in the world, terrorism must be eradicated. In the same year, 25,500 U.S. citizens were murdered (about forty-five percent of that total were handgun murders) and more than 50,000 people were killed on highways, forty percent of them due to drunk drivers (Clark 1993, 71). Most people perceive terrorism as more threatening to life, peace, and security than handgun ownership or highway travel. Yet the death rates as a result of terrorism, versus handgun and/or highway deaths, suggest just the opposite. What accounts for the disparity between the perceived threat and the actual threat of terrorism?

One possibility is that the definition of terrorism versus handgun or highway deaths leads to differences in perceived risk (see Zulaika and Douglas 1996). Highway travel and handgun ownership are viewed as normal, everyday occurrences and the risks of either activity are considered to be normal, perhaps expected. Deaths occurring as a result of either handgun ownership or highway travel are, therefore, also viewed as routine, small-scale events.

Most people rarely consider their place of work to be dangerous, even though anything from a fire to carbon monoxide poisoning can occur. So in 1995, when the Oklahoma City Federal Building was bombed killing nearly 200 employees and visitors, the event was front page news and the lead story on television for weeks. Ironically, during these weeks of news stories on the bombing, many more than two hundred people died as a result of car accidents and handgun murders. Even though interest groups such as the HCI (Handgun Control Inc.) or MADD (Mothers Against Drunk Drivers) and car insurance companies work hard to dramatize the number of handgun and highway accidents yearly, especially as a result of drunk drivers, these efforts do not begin to match the impact of an event defined as terrorism.

Another recent event defined as "terrorist" and heightening the level of fear and hostility toward terrorism in the United States was the dissemination of the Unabomber's publicized text, followed by the arrest of a suspect. The text was published in the same year as the Oklahoma City bombing, even though the Unabomber and the Unabomber's threats have existed for the last twenty years. Most people in the United States were not even aware of the "Unabomber" until 1995.[1] Incongruities in the actual and perceived social harm of terrorism as well as the historical timing or appropriateness for the propaganda of terrorism, should lead us to examine and understand the nature of the construct of terrorism and the conditions under which its perception and perpetuation become a matter of social import.

Why Study Terrorism?

Sociologists, in general, have avoided creating theories or analyses of terrorism, while political scientists have dominated the area (Crelinsten and Schmid 1995; Crenshaw 1995; Bell 1994; Shultz and Schmauder 1994; Wilkinson 1990 and 1986; Schmid and Jongman 1988; Stohl 1988; Gurr 1980; Jenkins 1979 and 1985). The avoidance by sociologists, however, has been for good reason (Gibbs 1989). Aside from the obvious problems associated with the ideological or political biases a definition or conceptualization of terrorism may promote, when we consider the expansive sociological literature on deviance and social control, from Durkheim to Foucault, terrorism can be examined heuristically as a form of deviance and/or social control.

As some researchers in the sociology of deviance have suggested, inherent in definitions of deviance and social control is a latent structure of politicality (see Lauderdale 1980 and Lauderdale and Cruit 1993; Ben-Yehuda 1990; Foucault 1979). It is this inherent politicality which makes possible the redefinition of an action, for example, from deviant to sick to conventional. The implications of this political approach to the study of deviance are far-reaching when we consider that the "deviants" or "normals" have the political potential to manipulate the definitions of their own and others' behavior. Terrorists and terrorism as a form of deviance and/or social control can be viewed from this interpretive theoretical framework. The old adage: "one person's terrorist is another person's freedom fighter" is a vulgar illustration of this point. The sociological approach can explicate the point by analyzing terrorism as an important construct in examining social and political processes of change and stability.

While most of the research on terrorism certainly recognizes this activity as an extreme form of coercive politics, knowledge about terrorism would benefit from a broader examination of the construct of terrorism rather than further conceptualizing or refining existing definitions of it. Just as the sociology of deviance has focused its attention on the construct of deviance by recognizing it as a relative rhetorical device that is socially negotiated, and on its various manifestations and their inherent politicality, so terrorism deserves to be examined in a systematic way. The task then becomes not to expose or define who the terrorist of the week is, whether it is the Unabomber threatening national security or the CIA conducting covert actions, but to examine the political processes and practices that maintain, create, and change the definitions of certain action as terrorist. Accordingly, we may be better able to understand the status of terrorism as either an act of deviance, social control, politics, and coercion or understand it in its particular time and place as a social problem (see Crenshaw 1995).

Text and Context: Italy and the U.S. as Sites of Struggle

According to most historical interpretations, violence has always existed, in varying degrees, within and among people. History repeatedly records and attempts to explain this phenomenon, usually in terms of winners and losers. All societies possess culturally constructed and socially organized processes for remembering and forgetting the past (see Geertz 1981). Symbolic forms, including narratives and stories, express the past and relate it in complex ways to present-day social interests. As such, they produce multiple, often conflicting, versions of the past and, at particular historical moments, may become sites of intense struggle. Such a historical moment appears to be present in a number of modern nation-states all over the world.

Incidents defined as terrorism often provide the script for historical interpretations of national identity and political sovereignty. The intense public fear of and hostility to terrorism produced by infrequent but dramatic incidents involves a complex process including interest group politics, the state, and the practices of a mass-mediated society: a process which has been explicated by Gramsci using the concept of hegemony (Gramsci 1971). For Gramsci, hegemony is produced via the practices of "institutions and organizations whose task it is to influence common sense" (Augelli and Murphy 1988, 24). Institutions such as education, media, and government organizations are involved in a process of generating information that appears simple and devoid of any intrinsic political problems or philosophical critiques. Teachers, for example, will often endlessly repeat certain simplified concepts to children until those concepts become part of a common, normal, "taken-for-granted" understanding.

Another practice involves the creation and implementation of political policies promoting socially accepted conventions combined with different and new interpretations. For example, Gramsci notes numerous instances from his own Italian society of state legislation that combined conventional Catholic conceptions (existing for centuries) with new Fascist programs (Caldwell 1986). Thus, hegemony, according to Gramsci, while referring to a dominant ideology, does not necessarily refer to a repressive process. Religious leaders, educators, government agents, legal and medical experts, researchers, and the media all partake in practices of disseminating and promoting certain dominant, paradigmatic interpretations of reality. And, of course, language and text as the vehicle by which to communicate and disseminate information is an inextricable part of this process of producing hegemony.

The Italian social and political milieu provided the empirical backdrop for Gramsci's theoretical formulation of hegemony. One of the most central and seemingly irreconcilable paradoxes that led Gramsci to develop the concept of hegemony was the unquestioned acceptance of a fascist, elitist regime by the largely peasant Southern Italian region during the twenties and thirties. This fundamental paradox spawned a number of contributing paradoxes, some of which juxtaposed Italian aestheticized representations of reality among literature, arts, theater, and public, national media (Gramsci 1966). The economic strife of the Southern Italian region, the needs as defined by the people, could not have logically predicted their allegiance to an elitist political system (Augelli and Murphy 1988; Mouffe 1979). Yet, some fifty years later, history would be fated to repeat itself, albeit under different circumstances.[2]

By the seventies, the Italian Communist Party had secured itself enough parliamentary seats to be a close second to the coalition, democratic government, composed of the Christian Democrats and Socialists. This time was also when "terrorist" activity was at its highest. Italy was in a constant state of "crisis" (*in crise*), which was a code expression for the combination of high unemployment, inflation, overpopulation, government instability, depleting natural resources, and violence plaguing the country. As the situation appeared to worsen, the communists would gain more votes and popularity. No one predicted the sudden decline of the communists at the height of their popularity, following the Red Brigades' "terrorist" action. And no one predicted Italy's adjustment to the stability of instability of its government. Yet, as Gramsci had noted many years earlier, Italian political culture (hegemony) thrived on paradox, as it provided the basis for competing interpretations of reality. And terrorist acts, rather than being viewed as a threat to the government, to the state, provided the catalysts for larger political changes. What had been considered a state of "crisis" in the seventies came to be perceived as a normal state of affairs for Italy, and incidents defined as terrorism provided a barometer for political change.

In the United States, great attention is devoted to the representation of national history, especially in the midst of its current cultural struggles; for example, attempts to commemorate the end of World War II have produced international controversies between the United States and various European societies as well as Japan. Attempts to commemorate the people involved in violent events such as war and terrorism via movies, documentaries, tourist attractions, and written and oral texts, have also produced a number of national and international struggles among these and other nation-states attempting to define their (multi)national heritages (see Goldberg 1994).

Currently, in the United States, institutional representations of historical events that developed during the nineteenth century and played a constitutive role in the formation of nation-states continue to exist. Nation-states often employ narration, drama, and stories to represent the present as the outcome of the pasts they construct. "It is the state which first presents a subject-matter that is not only adapted to the prose of History but involves the production of such History in the very progress of its own being" (Hegel 1970, 83). But the protagonists in this production are not only the obvious state agents and publicly funded organizations. Private museums, exhibitions, memorials, monuments to heroes, theme parks, historical films, and made-for-television mini-series provide visual (mis)representations of part of a nation's past (see Goldberg 1993, in particular page 160). In essence, history as construed and produced by professional researchers or scholars has become only one of many possible discourses on the past, and it has a limited hold on popular memory. Despite scholars' best attempts and intentions, unarguably in contemporary societies, the media are at the heart of the production of history. Violence represented as terrorism provides the dramatic script.

Events and the Production of Meaning

The collective remembering or forgetting of events, and the production of meaning, emerges from a complex process. The process becomes more evident in comparing two countries such as Italy and the United States, both typically represented as Western, technologically advanced societies.

Italy

One of the most decisive moments in Italian history, and the site of intense struggle, came in 1978 when Italian politician Aldo Moro was kidnapped, held hostage for fifty-five days, and then killed by the Red Brigades. Despite hundreds of violent confrontations with the Red Brigades, until that particular event, Italians had maintained a fairly indifferent attitude toward defining or describing this sort of violence by terms stronger than "extremism, subversivism, *squadrismo* [gangs] and *stragismo* [slaughterings]" (della Porta 1995, 106). It was viewed as just one more form of crisis in an already crisis-ridden political reality. As Wagner-Pacifici (1986, 2) notes about the Moro affair: "Its time (fifty-five days) and its spaces (newspaper pages, television screens, radio amplifiers, courtrooms, piazzas, walls) contained and encouraged competing interpretations and forms of discourse." Even piazzas and walls seemed to reflect popularized perceptions of media representations. Thus, this event provided the impetus for explanations of terrorism that were broad, encompassing the whole terrorist phenomenon.

This broad, competitive practice of political discussion and moral interpretation of the Moro affair by the Italian media reflected a certain social precedent regarding the public understanding of terrorism and the state responses to it. The process of socially negotiating the meaning and the actors of terrorism became a matter of overt public, political participation. Consequently, the interpretations presented during the unfolding and aftermath of the event actually gave the event its shape and meaning. By giving overt credit to certain interpretations while pronouncing others as faulty, the political, moral, and aesthetic meaning or quality of the interpretation was changed (Wagner-Pacifici 1986). Politics and power, for a brief historical moment, were socially recognized in the way Foucault (1979) recognizes them: as involved in the production of truth. As a result, the actors in the Moro affair while receiving an enormous amount of media attention, contributed to their own systematic demise as their interpretations of events were publicly falsified.

While no entity or group of persons emerged as the clear

winner in the Moro affair, what has become clear years later is the ability of the Italian state to, in a sense, absorb the so-called problem of terrorism and go on to define other social problems as the "real" cause of the unending Italian crisis. Despite numerous emergency laws, "special security" and counter-terrorist formations, repressive government action was for the most part ineffective. Such measures were deemed by the government itself as denying civil rights and ultimately as unconstitutional (della Porta 1995). Wagner-Pacifici (1986) analogously compares the ending of the Moro affair to a "mass suicide." The Red Brigades did not provide the catalyst for a massive class and ethnic struggle in Italy (as they had planned) through their most dramatic, systematic operation; rather, they provided a catharsis. Any such operations thereafter were anticlimactic. The very influential Communist Party became guilty by association. Despite the party's best attempts to dissociate from the Red Brigades, they were in the end viewed as a radical faction of the Communist party.[3] As Ben-Yehuda (1990, 15) notes, "a successful and enforceable social construction of a particular label of deviance depends on the ability of one or more groups to use or generate enough power so as to enforce their definition and version of morality on others." Neither the Red Brigades nor the Communist Party were successful at popularizing their interpretation of reality.

As for the state of the government, it was compromised by default. The government appeared to collapse in an immediate sense, and new leaders were elected. If there was any victor, it was compromise, which emerged as a de facto, assumed practice of the state, strengthening its structures in spite of its elected officials (Di Palma 1977).

But the story of "terrorism" in Italy goes beyond the Red Brigades, defined as Italy's notorious domestic terrorists, and includes "transnational" terrorists from the Middle East, Northern Africa, the Soviet Union, and Eastern Europe. Most of the media and government attention focused on the latter two areas, because left-wing terrorism was considered to be the greatest threat at this time and because of supposed connections with the Red Brigades. Yet groups, including the Armenians,

Libyans, and Palestinians, with ethnic ties to various Italian communities were also active during this time for their own national interests (Pisano 1987). Their violent activities did not become an issue for the media or government until the early eighties, and even then Italy was depicted more as a third-party battleground than a directly threatened national entity. Indeed, the kidnapping of American General James Dozier (which lasted about forty days), the killing of American diplomat Leamon Hunt, and the killing of Lando Conti, a mayor from Florence, did not have the same political impact as the Moro kidnapping. These latter actions, also conducted by the Red Brigades, were meant to be a direct attack against Italian/American and Italian/Israeli state relations. But by this time such action was anticlimactic and viewed as more of a Middle East/United States problem than an Italian one, despite the infamous actors of terrorism, the Red Brigades.

The process of competition and compromise among competing interpretations led to a ritualistic demise of the construct of terrorism. Indeed, since the Moro affair, even though numerous bombings, killings, and hostage takings have occurred in Italy, fewer and fewer have been officially defined as terrorism, nor have the Red Brigades been credited for such actions despite their continuing existence (compare with della Porta 1995; Pisano 1987). Terrorism, as a category of deviance, as a way of knowing, as a social problem, as a perceived threat against the stability of the nation-state, transcended all political boundaries of knowing, unravelled itself, and sealed its own doom.

The United States

At the present historical moment, the United States may be viewed as a site of intense discursive struggle over the construction and interpretation of its national past. Groups defined as subordinate, including racial, gender-based, religious, and issue-driven interest groups are challenging dominant representations of history. These include on-going challenges posed by American Indians reacting to the Columbus Day historical rendition and recent race riots in Los Angeles, reminding the public that thirty years after the second Civil Rights movement,

African Americans are still not treated equally or fairly by government social control agents and agencies (Inverarity *et al.*
1983). As a complex society, the United States is rich with different social groupings and diverse people. Maintaining the production of the past as a monolith is becoming increasingly difficult in a society where multiple and oftentimes conflicting
versions of the past exist simultaneously in place and space.
And while these larger struggles provide an index of hegemonic
crisis in the United States, terrorism is once again pictured as the
real crisis, the ostensible real threat to the stability of the nation-
state, the real enemy of national peace and security.[4]

Events of the recent past, including the New York Trade
Center bombing, the Oklahoma City federal building explosion,
the Unabomber attacks, or the Amtrack derailing, are events
deserving of indignant responses, but their definition and interpretation by the media and the state as homogeneous "terrorist"
events are grossly misleading. As in Italy thirty years ago, where
the world of terrorism was little more than a bewildering state
of affairs in an already crisis-ridden society until the Moro affair,
the United States appears to be undergoing its own struggle
with the world (or word) of terrorism in the midst of a much
broader and increasingly dangerous and violent social milieu.

These "waves" of social unrest and instability in the United
States are not without historical precedent. As Erikson (1966)
notes, for example, in the comparatively smaller, more homogeneous world of the Puritans in colonial America, the encroach-
ing heterogeneity, including different ethnicities, religious
worldviews, and gender roles, led to increasing threats and
challenges to the dominant order. These and related external
crises led to the witch hunts, which in the end were unsuccessful at preventing major political, economic, social turmoil and
change. Another historical period famous for social unrest was
the 1960s. This era of struggle saw the emergence of the counterculture movement: the hippies, yippies, and Black Panthers
within the social milieu of the Vietnam War. When the war
ended, the United States paid a price in economic and political
terms, much of which was blamed on the remanent "flower children" (who by this time were already a wilting species) for their

questioning of traditional structures and institutions such as gender roles, family structures, racism, and sexual preference (see Inverarity *et al.* 1983). Then, in 1995, we observed the reemergence of national scapegoating or "witch hunt" with regard to "terrorism," as U.S. President Clinton outlined his systematic, aggressive stand against it, which included executing the "terrorists." He stated on national television that "If this is not a crime for which capital punishment is called, I don't know what is." As the United States is involved in larger social struggles challenging hegemonic ideas concerning its national past, pride, and actions, events defined as "terrorist" appear to recur. The state turns to creating policies that expand its own visible means of violence, in order to name and justify its eradication of what it defines as the "real" destabilizing influence, the terrorists, in the name of restoring peace and stability (see Erikson 1966; Durkheim 1948).

The naming of "terrorist" activity captivated and overwhelmed the media and academic research after the Vietnam War, and in the 1990s we witness its reemergence. Terrorism may also be examined, in part, from a framework similar to the witch hunts, or the scapegoating of the counterculture. While the United States is currently the discursive site of major struggles involving its national and international identity, the focus is shifted to terrorism as the cause of social unrest. Yet there is another dimension to terrorism that warrants a more useful theoretical analysis.

Ben-Yehuda (1990, 3) examines complex societies in terms of "symbolic moral universes," or different and changing cultures within a larger "moral order" or state. He notes that: "the legitimization of power should be thought of in terms of a moral order that in turn defines the societal boundaries of different symbolic-moral universes." He further defines "direct and explicit acts that either challenge the social order or the abuse of power and morality by those in the centers" as "political deviance." Terrorist action may be broadly viewed in this way. Closer analysis, an analysis that considers terrorism as a "relative rhetoric" (also part of Ben-Yehuda's theory), views terrorism as a construct of the state or larger moral order. Terrorism may be viewed as an active part of statecraft in constituting nation-states and their continued sovereign stability. The question regarding the U.S. experience then becomes under what conditions is terrorism an index of, rather than the cause of or an explanation for, a deeper hegemonic crisis?

The Argument

It seems obvious enough that in all societies remembering and forgetting the past are culturally constructed and socially organized processes expressed through symbolic forms and displays and related in complex ways to present social interests (Geertz 1981). To examine these constructive processes, forms, and interests in a mass-mediated society as they produce different versions of reality is less obvious and less straightforward, however. An analysis of this sort defies most traditional approaches to research in the social sciences. Most approaches in the social sciences, for example, examine questions or interpretations about issues and incidents *a posteriori* for the purposes of arriving at some universal truths or generalizations. Consequently, contextual analyses are often rejected as relativistic or transitory and lacking in explanatory power. The present argument not only attempts to bring these two perspectives together in an analysis of terrorism, but also shows the futility of rejecting either perspective at the expense of the other.

As the producers of information and knowledge in the United States grapple once again with how to use the term "terrorism," and their focus becomes defining terrorism as groups or persons who are considered to be especially threatening to the site of legitimate violence, the state, it may be wise to examine how the discourse of terrorism has at other times, and regarding other incidents, been socially and politically negotiated and constructed. Consider the processes of political and rhetorical negotiation in two crucial incidents, the *Achille Lauro* affair and TWA hijacking and their unfolding drama(s) in two sites of interpretive struggle. This study provides an examination of the *Achille Lauro* and TWA incidents as a reference for how the unfolding drama(s) of recent and future outbreaks of violence may be defined, constructed, and understood.

Unlike many earlier works on terrorism, the focus of inquiry in this study is not to more clearly define terrorism in terms of different state interpretations. Rather, its analytical eye centers on the discourse or rhetoric of terrorism surrounding two specific incidents, the *Achille Lauro* affair (1985) and the TWA (1985) hijacking. It also focuses upon two different discourses of terrorism surrounding these two incidents—U.S. and Italian. Each discourse re-presents the state. As this study shows, the term, terrorism, does not even exist in the regional dialects of the latter country despite its existence in the state language. This study argues that the representational practices of the texts not only shaped definitions, knowledge, and public perceptions bearing on these events themselves but also contextualized (both geographically and historically) the roles their countries were playing in international politics. The term, terrorism, allowed for the specific construction of ideological and political boundaries. It further discusses how these representational practices were complemented by technological practices, such as simulation and speed, that allowed highly complex communications networks to collect, store, organize, and instantly transmit these representations over great distances.

As a plethora of social science experts conducting research on terrorism are dredged up to further define or refine the concept of terrorism, it is imperative to remember that the bombing of the World Trade Center in New York City, the killing of two CIA agents just outside the agency's headquarters, or the bombing in Oklahoma City are not the only outbreaks of violence in the United States that have invoked terror, thereby being terrorist in nature. On the contrary, violent activity occurs daily, at different levels of analysis, from the private home to the public organization, especially within technologically advanced societies. And if we examine the development of the concept of terrorism in the eighteenth and nineteenth centuries, we further note that the fundamental controlling apparatus of the state (as the site of legitimate violence) is based largely on terrorism. Yet, if we continue to accept what most social scientific knowledge about terrorism has taught us, it will continue to be not only a misunderstood phenomenon but also a particularly unnerving form of violence, seemingly impervious to any form of social control.

A number of premises form the basis of my inquiry into the state of terrorism. These premises integrate promising directions for analyses derived in part from critical, symbolic interaction, and neo-functionalist perspectives with contextual analysis, the analysis of text and discourse:

1. Inherent in constructions and definitions of terrorism is a latent structure of politicality that allows for practices that maintain, create, and change its definition (or the definition of certain action as terrorist) to some other label;
2. Societies possess culturally constructed and socially organized processes for remembering and forgetting the past and defining the present. Modern, complex societies often produce multiple versions of the past and at particular historical moments, they may become sites of intense struggle;
3. The United States is currently undergoing a particular historical moment of intense struggle and hegemonic crisis; terrorism, a term developed in the eighteenth and nineteenth centuries to represent the interests of the nation-state and its sovereignty becomes a focus of discursive struggle;
4. In Italy, terrorism as a site of discursive struggle for monolithic representations has seen its twilight, privileging heterogeneous understandings that the state views as secondary and unthreatening to its essential identity, structure, and survival;
5. Terrorism may be viewed as a relative rhetoric intrinsic to the process or art of statecraft. It is a discursive practice in the constitution of nation-states and their continued sovereign stability and expansion.

The Plan

My intention in this study is to explore, examine, and expand on research that explicates the processes and practices of discourse involved in normalizing or naturalizing the meaning of terrorism (see Zulaika and Douglas 1996; Wagner-Pacifici 1986; de Lauretis 1985). Examining these constructive processes, forms, and interests in a mass-mediated society as they produce different versions of reality is less distinct. The methodological framework must lead to an interpretive analysis that can explicate often elusive practices of language under certain social and historical conditions.[5]

While most previous research on terrorism has attempted to construct, redefine, refine, and elaborate upon a variety of existing conceptualizations and models and interpretive frameworks for its analysis, this study does not. Such research has been very useful and successful at fixing a meaning to terrorism by defining its causes, consequences, communities, and countermeasures. Crelinsten and Schmid (1995, 3) list some of the various motives of academics for conducting (or not conducting) empirical research on political torture, a manifestation of "terrorism." Whatever the motivation, and despite an extensive body of knowledge on terrorism, it would appear that especially in the United States, terrorist activity is ostensibly on the rise rather than in decline.

Perhaps the apparent rise of terrorism today in the United States has more to do with the nature of the dominant and available information produced, including definitions, conceptualizations, models, and typical scientific paradigms. In *Wayward Puritans,* Erikson (1966, 22) suggests that "men who fear witches soon find themselves surrounded by them; men who become jealous of private property soon encounter eager thieves." Following Erikson's logic, it stands to reason that men who fear "terrorists" soon find themselves surrounded by them.

This is not to say that incidents such as the bombing of a federal building or the Unabomber's actions are not worthy of condemnation. Or that the violence at Waco and Ruby Ridge is not worth further investigation. But under what conditions are these incidents and actions defined as "terrorism" instead of something else such as political violence or simply murder? And what are the practices by which such meaning is fixed and viewed as normal?

The premise that interpretation—the imposition of concepts, models, and frameworks—is intimately and actively involved in fixing the meaning of terrorism, publicly acknowledged as real and true, is my analytical point of departure. The process of fixing meaning where meaning is intrinsically among the contested political states, is one of the phenomena to be examined. My interest, then, is not to decide which definitions, discourses, or state interpretations of terrorism are better or more reflective of "truth" and provide empirical support for them. To do so would be implicitly to proffer a promise: a promise that my research would work to settle and discipline ambiguities and paradoxes regarding the discourse of terror by constructing (or improving upon) new and powerful boundaries or truths. I make no such promise. To do so would also implicitly sustain a certain fixed nature regarding theory and analysis, thus depriving theory and analysis of their ability to be "reflective," to ask "how" such theories became constructed in the first place (Mills 1959). My own practice in this exploration of discourse is, paradoxically, an interpretive one. Thus, interpretation as a play of power in providing meaning, a meaning in which the author and the reader may be considered as occupying the same sovereign standpoint, the same center of interpretation, is a primary analytical concern. The tensions and paradoxes emerging from my analysis, rather than being looked upon as troubling, are invited and valued, as they open up possibilities for further analysis.

The latter statement, not surprisingly, may present a conundrum with respect to the present text: how does one treat the text that describes the phenomenon? In general, any text that makes "paradox" one of its central analytical themes should itself be openly examined for the paradoxes it suggests. With respect to the research provided by this text, however, it is one thing to claim that the interpreter shapes others' apprehension of events. It is another thing to credibly demonstrate this process. The juxtaposition of the textual and contextual approaches becomes essential to studying terrorism in the art of statecraft.

In this research, terrorism and the state are assumed to be symbiotically related. Thus, the discourse of terrorism is inextrica-

bly related to the art of statecraft (see Tilly 1985). Of analytical significance are the conditions under which modes of subjectivity—
the state and its relation to terror—become modes of objectivity,
i.e., the production of hegemony (Foucault 1979; Gramsci 1971).

One of the ways in which modes of subjectivity become
modes of objectivity is via the text. My examination will focus
on texts spawned by the *Achille Lauro* and TWA incidents—texts
that were involved in the process of shaping public knowledge
about terrorism in both Italy and the United States. As both societies use and are used by the media, whether it pertains to news,
scholarly works, or government reports, these texts must be
considered as discursive resources available in both locations.

Certainly, upon a glance, we can note that these texts reveal
different aesthetics and different dispositions. Their cultural
descendancies informed by different social and historical contexts are obvious. When differences can be observed between
the two societies in the way an incident is represented, however,
what becomes important is not the banal reification of those differences but how they are produced and sustained as differences. The social and historical conditions under which certain
practices or *modi operandi* are sustained, as well as the different
modi operandi themselves, become of crucial analytical significance. The ways in which some actions come to be regarded as
terrorist is the focus, vis-à-vis the successful crediting or discrediting of interpretations, the suppression of certain interpretations and the highlighting of others, the ideological direction
of certain interpretations, as well as the overall perspective of
the public and its participation and/or celebration of the
process of statecraft.

My purpose, however, is not to confirm the differences
between the two societies, as if certain cultural imperatives
stand above and dictate the workings of the societies themselves. Nor do I intend to assert that the strategies involved in
the definition of terrorism are not interchangeable or shared in
the interpretation of other events in these societies. Rather, the
focus is on the practical production of social and political constructions of terrorism. Such a focus is useful for questioning
and expanding existing theories on terrorism. In larger measure,

though, its value is in enabling the questioning and reconsideration of political processes crucial to democracy, namely the celebration of differences, diversity, and open debate.

Because my aim is to investigate how the rhetorical strategies in the discourse of terrorism are produced, sustained, transformed, or suppressed, as well as the practical, political action such rhetoric prescribes, a semiotic approach is heuristic. In a semiotic analysis, language is usually analyzed as a sign system within the typical, taken-for-granted, grammatical-linguistic categories of words, sentences, phrases. As a sign system, it may take several sentences to interpret a particular meaning, or meaning may be interpreted from those words and phrases that are left out, silenced, or repressed (Namaste 1993; Armstrong 1985; Merrell 1985; Eco 1979; Barthes 1977; Nilsen 1977; Saussure 1916). Such an analysis looks beyond the meaning contained within the limits of the categories and rules defined by linguistics, and attempts to interpret the meaning contained within the forms, orders, and structures in which they are presented. It is sensitive to the politics of writing, including the author in authority. And few constructs are as misunderstood as terrorism in their "meaning potential," the inextricable link between knowledge and the production of power via the detailed descriptions, categorizations, and hierarchical organizations of contemporary society (Ben-Yehuda 1996; Namaste 1993). Thus, distinctions between terror and rhetoric and the institutions that support such distinctions must necessarily be considered. A semiological approach allows the researcher to be less concerned with the text's objectivity, reliability, or "honesty." White (1987, 192) aptly writes that one is able to examine its

> ideological aspect less as a product . . . than as a process. It permits us more precisely, to regard ideology as a process by which different kinds of meaning are produced and reproduced by the establishment of a mental set towards the world in which certain sign systems are privileged as necessary, even natural, ways of recognizing a "meaning" in things and others are suppressed, ignored, or hidden in the very process of representing a world to consciousness.

Such a process occurs within all types of writing, whether literary, poetic, or scientific (see Gusfield 1976). The rhetoric of science, for example, utilizes a specific sign system or code for that which it attempts to represent, and such a process indeed affects how we read these texts. White (1973, 27) has also argued that:

> [T]he ethical moment of a historical work [is] reflected in the mode of ideological implication by which an aesthetic perception (the emplotment) and a cognitive operation (the argument) can be combined so as to derive prescriptive statements from what may appear to be purely descriptive or analytical ones.

Semiology focuses attention on the layers of meaning that may be embodied in a simple set of representations. The signifier, or word(s) in the case of this research, and the signified, the mental picture or meaning indicated by the signifier, produce a sign that is the association or relationship established between them. While some relationships may be very direct, others are considerably more complex because of their arbitrariness. As a sign system, semiology is sensitive to the political meaning(s) and paradoxes of social practice that often elude traditional scientific approaches. Signs can communicate latent and manifest meanings as well as define moral values and generate feelings and attitudes in the reader. If we are to study the "latent structure of politicality" inherent in definitions of terrorism, that rhetorical structure allowing for its reconstruction, suppression, or even demise (both rhetorically and practically), such an approach is essential (Lauderdale 1980).

It is important, however, to note that this study compares two separate incidents (nearly the same sort of event and occurring at nearly the same time), rather than alternative interpretations of the same incident, for substantive theoretical reasons. Typically, the process of deconstruction in a semiotic analysis involves the comparison of what is signified with alternative "paradigms" not chosen. The "natural" comparison would be between such paradigms in Italy and the United States as alternative interpretations of the same incident. Yet this study also

examines the intellectual descendancy and theoretical orientation of the present construct of terrorism, explicitly demonstrat-
ing its inextricable link to statecraft in ensuring the sovereignty
and authority of the nation-state. Trans World Airlines (TWA) is
a U.S. airline corporation. The *Achille Lauro* is an Italian ship.
Passengers from many different nation-states were being trans-
ported by each of these carriers, including Italian and U.S. citizens. Even though the seizure of each of these carriers was
defined as an international event or threat, the retaliatory
responses were still the responsibility of the respective nation-
states. Each nation-state responded differently to structurally
similar attacks. This difference provides examples of the "signified" (the dominant definition of terrorism as used in the United
States) as compared to alternatives not chosen (the desuetude of
the term in Italy). The same terms or signifiers, with the potential for similar representations, are signified differently—in
accordance with different state (political) interests.

Having said all this, it hardly seems appropriate to refer to
a "method" of analyzing discourse or to my method of analysis
as though the method stands above the analysis as a neutral,
apolitical medium with which to grasp and report upon the
external world. As this is an interpretive work in and of itself,
the question of method becomes an integral part of how the
analysis unfolds, one that itself is open to debate and critique.
The theme of having a method, an apolitical, neutral method, in
certain respects is among the practices examined in the politics
of these texts. To be sure, my analysis of the discourses surrounding the *Achille Lauro*/TWA events takes seriously certain
metaphors that are viewed as participating in the fixing of
meaning on terrorism, and that are drawn upon not only in the
texts to be analyzed but also in my text. To be sure, too, the
metaphor of "method" is among the metaphors analyzed. But
my analytical plan in this study does not claim a method of its
own; it does not defer to a putative authoritative ground that
can arbitrarily constrain the meanings determined in this study.

As many of the texts on the *Achille Lauro* and TWA incidents from both sides of the Atlantic appear to exploit the notion
of terrorism as "theater," this metaphor appeared appropriate as

a way of themetizing my interrogations of these texts. Not only does this metaphor emerge from the texts themselves, but it invites questions that cut across a variety of disciplinary fields.[6] In understanding the rhetoric of terror and/or the terror of rhetoric, I also exploit the aesthetic dimensions of the theater typically used in both societies to emphasize certain aspects of the "terrorist" phenomenon. The "theater" form, therefore, gives shape not only to the typical descriptions and explanations of terrorism in both societies but also to the content and the political agendas implied therein. Thus, for representation reasons, the analysis will take on the various features and codes of a theater or stage production such as plot, characterization, theme(s), props and stunts, and the audience-actor relationship (compare with Wagner-Pacifici 1986). By analyzing the discourse of terrorism within the aesthetic/theatrical reality it is generally granted and by applying the line of reasoning inherent in a semiological/textual orientation, we can explore how and the conditions under which various theatrical metaphors, structural codes, literary genres, and narrative modes are reflected in texts, as well as what effect these have on the public's response both to the text itself and the ideological context in the text.

Also, my selection of mass-mediated materials in addition to more specialized research texts reflects interest in exploring how discourse understanding and significant knowledge is grounded and disseminated beyond academic settings (see Ericson, Baranek, and Chan 1991; deLauretis 1985; Eco 1979; Avalle 1970). The general availability of texts from prominent magazines, newspapers, government reports, and academic writings guided the selection of texts to be analyzed in this study. Texts from newspapers such as *Avanti* and *Corriere della Sera*, for example, were selected as much because they represent two of the major political party protagonists involved in the Italian theater of terrorism, because of high circulation rates and availability. Most of the texts are available from public or university libraries in the United States and Italy; however, many of the government transcripts were made available to me through the Consulato Generale d'Italia in the United States. Also, the

Catholic Church, especially in Italy, was of invaluable help. Unlike libraries where smaller newspapers are not saved and catalogued, the Church provides elaborate cataloguing systems for them (dating from the early seventies), stored on microfilm and fiche. Furthermore, because most of the Italian texts (with the exception of Cassese 1989 and Judges of Genoa transcripts 1985) were not translated, I provide my own translations to facilitate the analysis.[7]

In general, the discourse of terrorism as exemplified in mass media texts will be analyzed in terms of their political practice, as a rhetorical form of power politics. Media discourse that endeavors to construct, define, and conceptualize reality is engaged in the active interpretation, production, normalization, and resistance of modes of imposed order, modes of structuring social existence. The various strategies of discourse discussed in this study will be viewed as viable, subjective, linguistic strategies by which social and political practice is disciplined, normalized, and perpetuated within society. Accordingly, we may explore the practical, political production of reality through the "conventional" language we hear and read daily in the media and, in the case of this study, the social reality constituting terrorism and violence in society (White 1987; Gramsci 1966).

2

WRITING THE SCRIPT:
LANGUAGE, HEGEMONY,
AND HISTORICAL INTERPRETATION

Researchers and scholars throughout this century have been interested in exploring the centrality of language as it shapes and organizes perceptions of reality. Philosophers, social scientists, and natural scientists have increasingly recognized language as elemental not only in shaping and relaying ideas, but also as it relates to how we think about and perceive the essence of the world. As Wittgenstein (1921, 83–85) notes: "An investigation of the structure of language is at the same time an investigation of the formal aspects of the world. To give the essence of propositions means to give the essence of all description, therefore the essence of the world" (see also Polsky 1991; Gusfield 1976; Heidegger 1971; Chomsky 1959; Whorf 1956; Saphir 1929).

The symbiotic relationship between the state and terrorism leads to a consideration of sociological, anthropological, ideological, and epistemological assumptions upon which these constructions are based. The construct of terrorism as it is used in contemporary research and popular texts emerges from eighteenth- and nineteenth-century orthodox assumptions of man, nation-state, and political sovereignty. Inherent in textual constructions of terrorism, therefore, are definite ideological, anthropological, and epistemological assumptions about men and women, (as well as other cultural groups and classes), their social and political natures and relations. These assumptions provide prescriptive attitudes and responses to institutions such as the state (compare with Thomas *et al.* 1987). Paradoxically, an outmoded construct of terrorism is used pervasively today, in a world that has challenged (and continues to challenge) orthodox beliefs about "man," nation-state and political sovereignty. And, the state, while recognizing its own changes in constitution, still reserves the discursive meaning and political power of this construct.

The practice of discourse as a form of power and action, especially with respect to the discourse of terrorism, is a territory that has received insufficient attention by researchers. It is considered to eschew grand theories, which attempt to conceptualize, define, and/or control the production of knowledge (Namaste 1993). To analyze terrorism from a discursive attitude is considered to be threatening because it blurs categories of knowing, conceptual definitions of what is and is not terroristic, and practices of securing identity, which are necessary to the production of hegemony whether identity is constructed at individual, national, or international levels (Sassoon 1987; Gramsci 1971). A more critical position against examining dominant categories of knowing resuscitates the dangers inherent in relativist Nietzschean-type themes, which have been used politically to legitimate fascist social practices. As Antonio (1995, 29) notes:

> The political directions of Nietzscheanism's highly aestheticized anti-bourgeois, antidemocratic, and irrationalist themes are highly ambiguous and pliable. Georges Sorel employed them in arguments about the purifying powers of violence, war and mass mobilization.... After the war, as Aschheim holds, the "mythologized Germanic Nietzsche" became the most important source of inspiration, vision and intellectual legitimation for the resurgent radical right.

Yet discursive practices are an integral, indispensable part of political practice and the practices of power. In a mass-mediated society where social, economic, and moral life is informed by an endless procession of aestheticized interpretations via rhetoric, images, and signs, such elusive practices indeed intervene in the creation of social theory and political policy (Namaste 1993;

Foucault 1979). And in the case of "terrorism" as it is understood and predominantly known in research and society, it is
only a relativistic, discursively produced conception. Definitions of terrorism based on polemics abound (Crenshaw 1995;
Brown and Merrill 1993; compare with Gibbs 1989). The "brute
existence" that "escapes categorization in language," as when,
for example, one searches "for the words to describe some inar-
ticulate feeling or sensation . . ."(Nash 1994, 73) is not captured
in the dominant definitions of terrorism, i.e., the sensations felt
by those who experience terror daily, from domestic to environmental violence. Furthermore, although dominant definitions of
terrorism are not grounded in social theory, it has not stopped
unreflective social scientists from building on their already scientifically questionable foundations and providing an entire
politically relativistic body of knowledge on the subject.[1] Under
these conditions, it is not surprising that those who produce this
type of research on terrorism would be the first to condemn and
incite fear of discursive analyses or reject them completely.

Terrorist activity occurs daily, at different levels of analysis,
especially within technologically advanced societies and societies whose structures, institutions, and organizations privilege
hierarchy and domination.[2] When terrorism is theoretically
examined as a form of social control, fundamental controlling
apparatuses of the state may be viewed as terroristic. Organizations, groups, and individuals who legitimate the use of violence to achieve their goals may be viewed as products of, exten-
sions of, or models of the essential structure of a state when its
purpose is to regulate behavior via various forms of repression,
domination, and terror.

Such a theoretical view of the state, its structure, and its
ultimate survival is critically relevant, because the construct of
terrorism typically is adopted discursively by the state to represent threats against its sovereignty. One of the main reasons why
"terrorism" is most usefully examined as a discursive practice is
because of its intellectual descendancy. The disparity between
perceived and actual social harm produced by such action and
represented in its discourse is understandable (but no less paradoxical) when terrorism is examined as a descendent of classic

nineteenth-century thought, including the paradigms and conceptual referents of that age as well as within a rhetorical theory of knowledge (Stehr 1994; Foucault 1979).

The Intellectual Descendancy of Terrorism

From the late 1960s to the present, considerable research has emerged on terrorism, defining or describing it. Most of the language surrounding terrorism assumes it to be not only a recent phenomenon, but also a special type of phenomenon (within which occur many subtypes) worthy of examination and explication in its own right. But the construct of terrorism as it is used in contemporary research and politics is a descendent of classic intellectual nineteenth-century thought. Indeed, the construct of terrorism today is little different (typically not at all) from the way it is used in Edmund Burke's *Reflections on the Revolution in France,* written in 1790. In this work, Burke refers to the revolutionary spirit of the French democratic movements as terrorism. Contemporary conceptualizations of terrorism may be examined appropriately as derivatives of the discourse emerging from and reflective of nineteenth-century social theories and realities (Stehr 1994; Foucault 1972 and 1979).

The construct of terrorism includes the paradigms and conceptual referents from the age out of which it emerged. The construct of terrorism calls upon certain ideological understandings of "man," his anthropological and social nature, and his relationship to societal institutions such as the state (compare with Oliverio and Desjardins 1993; Connell 1985; deLauretis 1985). One of the most important referents of the social realities and social theories at this time, for example, is man as subject and author of the universe. Another important and related referent is the nation-state demarcated by territorial boundaries and its sovereign survival. For this reason (and more complex ones examined below), when the contemporary U.S. State Department identifies Syria, Iraq, Libya, Algeria, and North Korea to be among the major supporters of terrorism in the world today, images of domestic violence as terrorism are not predominant in a society's political consciousness (see Petras 1987 and Huggins 1987).

Burke's *Reflections* is a searching inquiry into the nature of reform and revolution. He focuses his examination on the French Revolution in devising a course of political action and a style of political writing capable of countering the threat of revolution, which he perceives as terroristic. He often exposes us directly to the source of the terror and "fuels those passions he considers most likely to quell it" (Reid 1985, 85). Burke was quick to realize that the Revolution was more than an internal French affair, that it was a "revolution of doctrine and theoretic dogma" (Ebenstein 1969, 230). As such, in order to provide an effective counterrevolutionary response, *Reflections* is written in a grand-style political rhetoric. However, at the same time, Burke does not respond as though the Revolution were an awesome, inspiring event. On the contrary, he mobilizes a kind of rhetoric of terror in order to alert his readers to the perils of the situation. He attacks the state that emerged from the revolution as a "college of armed fanatics, for the propagation of the principles of assassination, robbery, fraud, faction, oppression and impiety" (Ebenstein 1969, 235). In identifying the movement as fanatic, Burke summons a European crusade to crush, by force of arms, the revolutionary spirit of democracy.

The relevance of analyzing the discourse of terrorism in Burke's work is that it reflects the references of man, and by extension, man as a unit of analysis in the production of knowledge and hegemony at this time. The subject or typical man to whom Burke speaks and who is the "spectator" of the fanaticism and terror of the French Revolution is a representative of the English gentry. His belief in man as the central subject and author of the universe, divinely ordered and ordained, is central to his view and conception of terrorism. With the exception of the aristocratic male, he asserts that all other people, while undeserving of oppression, nevertheless ought to stay in their places. Burke's writing reflects the notion that man is politically significant, not as an individual citizen, but solely as a member of a group to which he belongs socially or economically. In this respect, he accepts his own inferiority to those whom he believes are the repository of political wisdom and experience.

Just as the conception of aristocratic man as subject and

author of the universe was being threatened by the "terrorist" movements of the day, i.e., the idea that working-class men be allowed to vote and ideals of democracy as the rule of the masses, so too, the ideal of the nation-state and its sovereign survival was under increasing threat. The political theories of the nineteenth century, especially theories and critiques of liberal democracy, maintained as central the notion of the nation-state as the identity of society, its sovereign survival including the survival of the social system (Stehr 1994; Held 1989). As Stehr (1994, 21) suggests,

> Obviously there may have been and perhaps still are some good reasons for the identification of the boundaries of the social system with those of the nation-state. For example, the formation of social science discourse to some extent coincides with the constitution of the identity of the modern nation-state and violent struggles among nation-states.

The dominant ideal of statesmanship at this time is represented as avoiding the extremes of either tearing down the existing order or resisting change. This view of the appropriate, normal behavior of a statesman is explicated in contrast to the state emerging from the French Revolution, which is defined as threatening. The reforms of the French Revolution are viewed as innovations derived from a selfish temper and narrow views. They are defined as crude, harsh, terroristic, mixed with imprudence and injustice, and contrary to human institutions.

In defining terrorism, threats to the sovereignty of the nation-state are not acknowledged as being the result of deep-seated historical conflicts and forces, but rather as the incorrect doctrines of philosophers who were animated by fanatical atheism and the vile ambitions of politicians driven by an opportunistic lust for power. In *Reflections*, Burke is particularly vehement in his denunciation of French philosophers such as Rousseau and Voltaire and other similar men of letters, calling them robbers, assassins, bandits, and terrorists. Their ideologies were viewed as inspiring feelings of discontent among the masses. The idea of democracy or the tyranny of multitudes was at this time viewed as a state of terror by those states wanting to preserve monarchical rule, the church's idea of misery as a blessing for the masses, and aristocracy as divinely ordained. By those who opposed innovative social constructions, Rousseau and Voltaire were defined not only as treasonous but also as mentally disordered (Ebenstein 1969).

Edmund Burke's *Reflections* represents the status quo views of man and nation-state at a time when both conceptions were being challenged and threatened. The expansion of the term "man" to include all men, rather than just aristocratic men, and the increasing threats to colonial rule were seen as undermining the "normal" order of society and state. Any action levelled against that state was defined as terrorism. Today the construct of terrorism is given multifaceted meaning in representing the politics of the contemporary nation-state in international politics. Yet what has remained constant is the construct's reference to acts undermining the state and its re-presentative institutions and organizations in society as terrorism. Despite increasing economic and environmental globalization, gender politics and the resurgence of nationalities within territorial boundaries, the discourse of terrorism, as a practice of the state in the art of statecraft, is still crucial to the construction of political boundaries.[3]

A New Definition for an Old Construct

Within the last thirty years, terrorism has developed into a field of study in its own right, with its own experts who specialize in knowing and identifying terror.[4] Most contemporary research on and knowledge of terrorism is similar to Burke's representative work focusing on explaining why certain actors engage in a particular type of action (see Lauderdale and Inverarity 1980). Suggesting the intent or motivation of such actors and their actions draws clear boundaries around notions of what is and is not terrorist action in society. Profiles of terrorists, commonly written by today's experts in the area, provide an example of the construction of the definition of terrorism—they define the who, what, and why of terrorism (Arendt 1969;

Hacker 1976; Goldaber 1979; Jenkins 1979; Schmid and Jongman 1988; Handler 1990; Wilkinson 1986 and 1990; Crenshaw 1983 and 1995; Sharif 1996). Explaining "why" certain action occurs, therefore, assumes a non-diverse order in society much as in Burke's eighteenth-century writings. It has become an important part in the process of establishing a collective definition of terrorist action (compare with Gramsci 1971). Such knowledge about terrorism (as well as other categories of deviance and social control) further shapes and is shaped by a wider institutional and societal order (Thomas *et al.* 1987). In this regard, Ericson, Baranek, and Chan (1987, 29) note that:

> [T]he ideological labour of reproducing social, cultural, political, and economic order is not simply a matter of vacuous theorizing by academics interested in the political economy of the state. It is a matter of major concern to the state . . .

Scholarly explanations of terrorism, therefore, are central to the creation of laws and policies because they re-present similar "techniques of policing and moral brokerage," as well as

> direct or encourage journalists to work on behalf of the established order. Journalists are officially defined as crucial agents in the reproduction of order . . . an instrument for the defence of our identity as a nation. (Ericson, Baranek, and Chan 1987, 29 and 1991, 8)

It is not surprising that texts, whether they are generated by scholars, politicians, or news media, as the bearers of knowledge/power can be viewed as contributing to (and/or reproducing) social stratification, integration, social order, and, of course, hegemony. As such, "It is the organization of news, not events in the world, that creates news" (Ericson, Banarek, and Chan 1987, 345).

The primary difference between nineteenth century's and today's representations of terrorism is the dominance of an ostensible scientific discourse in today's explanation. The dominant discourse that shapes contemporary knowledge and meaning on terrorism is a legacy of eighteenth- and nineteenth-century discourse of logic and reason. The indistinguishable identity between society and nation-state during this time of history was an integral part of the emergence and construction of social science discourse (Stehr 1994). Scientific discourse is projected as a monolith containing and reflecting objective truth. Other discourse is usually relegated to the realms of polemic or fiction. Without the development of a facade of detached reason and logical arguments (often accompanied by convenient data and figures), contemporary analysis of social reality often is not viewed as serious research. Thus, most contemporary knowledge on terrorism, in form, attempts to offer conceptualizations and theoretical parameters for empirical analyses.[5] It is crucial, however, to explicate the form of the explanations, as the form of the discourse represents and shapes the dominant political values, relations, and references of the historical period (see Gusfield 1976; Foucault 1979; Stehr 1994).

The subject or typical person for whom modern research on terrorism is written is not representative of the English gentry, it is the worldly, cosmopolitan, middle-class figure of man. Thus, terrorists are not to be identified simply by class, a class other than or inferior to aristocracy, but by a more diverse set of categories representative of the challenges to cosmopolitan, middle-class males, i.e., those who are presented as the potential victims of terrorism. For this reason, research on terrorism identifies many different types of terrorists including ethnic-nationalist, ideological, religious, issue, and state, to name a few (Sharif 1996; Schmid and Jongman 1988; Shank 1987). Each type of terrorism is defined in relation to its challenge or threat to the normal order or conception (assumptive standard) of "normal" people living in a "normal" society (Foucault 1979). Despite the many different possible types of terrorism identified and defined in modern research, much as in Burke's work, the term is still used to define action viewed as threatening to assumptions and conceptions of the status quo, the politics at large, or what Gramsci refers to as the universal subjective.

The universal subjective, briefly, involves the interpretation of superstructural categories and principles consensually shared and actively guiding the practices of those categories (Ashley 1984). In short, the universal subjective is the production of hegemony. The term, terrorism, is therefore an interpretive political construct emerging from the understandings of the superstructure and is actively involved in the construction of reality, the shaping of a world, and the shaping of its subjects. The subjects of this world, whether it is Burke's or today's world, will objectively come to know "terrorism" as a practice that is other to themselves—a practice that must be regulated, limited, or suppressed by those who possess the legitimate means of coercion, violence (Gramsci 1971).

Ironically, the standard of the state as represented in contemporary research on terrorism is the state that Burke attempts to undermine in his writings by calling it a terrorist state, that is, a liberal democratic nation-state. Yet the processes of the liberal democratic ideal are now assumed to be legitimate. Even analyses of state terror focus on the wrongdoing of a state, rather than the state as an imposed institution in society vested with the legitimate means of violence (see Kressel 1996). We come to know what the legitimate liberal democratic nation-state is by being presented with a comparison to "other" categories of states such as socialist, radical democratic, authoritarian, militaristic, revolutionary, or "underdeveloped."

In contemporary discussions of terrorism, many different "types" of nation-states are defined and measured against the standard of the ideal liberal democratic state. Each type of state presents certain conditions most conducive to particular types of terrorism. In his discussion of state terrorism, for example, Stohl (1988, 201) notes the following:

> The first of those aspects is the extent to which agents of the state have employed strategies of terrorism in their mix of methods of governance. Although we recognize exceptions, we summarize the picture as one in which the heaviest use of state terrorism occurred in immediately postrevolutionary Second World [*sic*] societies, followed all too closely by many Third World [*sic*] societies in the contem-

porary era. . . . As a rule, First World [*sic*] governments
make relatively little use of terror as a means of governance, although it is not unheard of even in that context.

Clearly, the above passage presents the U.S. system with respect
to "other" systems via the practice of "terrorism" defined as illegitimate, ultimately undermining the authority of the state and
its practice of legitimate forms of violence. In his ostensibly
objective, analytical, and scientific presentation, Stohl has quite
effectively constructed for us a view, a conception of the legitimate means of violence, of the nation-state as it shall come to be
known and respected (Weber 1954 and 1958).

Wilkinson (1990, 1) in a similar vein, authoritatively states
that:

[A]mong scholars of all disciplines who have studied political violence it is generally accepted that terrorism is a special form of political violence . . . a weapon or method
which has been used throughout history by both states and
sub-state organizations for a whole variety of political
causes or purposes.

Terrorism as a construct is given an objective formation because
it is accepted by most scholars as a special form of political violence. The dominating perspective is equated with "truth."
Alternative explanations of this phenomenon would simply be
considered as erroneous if they do not reflect the *dominant* scholarly views of the day. Wilkinson (1990, 2) also attempts to place
his theoretical orientation of terrorism within a historical legacy
of anticolonial struggles, from the Sicarii and Zealots against the
Roman occupation to the European colonial rule of World War
II (with the exception of the American struggle against Britain in
the 1700s). He then goes on to claim that:

[T]he *real* burgeoning of modern international terrorism
did not occur until the end of the 1960s. International incidents of terrorism have increased tenfold since 1968 and
now directly affect, to some degree, over half the countries

in the international system. What are the underlying causes and implications of this iniquitous *modern* form of political violence? (*emphasis mine*)

Is it or is it not a uniquely modern form of violence? What appears to be unique about terrorism is the conditions under which this construct is employed to obscure rather than sharpen our analyses of politics and power. Yet, despite the content of Wilkinson's ideological stance on the world of terrorism, the structure of his explanations make one relationship abundantly clear: that terrorism is a discursive practice in the art of state-craft. Crenshaw (1995, 9) notes that "a label is a useful short-hand, combining descriptive, evocative and symbolic elements, but its meanings are inherently flexible and ambiguous. They may even be contradictory." She also acknowledges the pre-scriptive implications of such rhetorical forms and definitions as an essential part of political processes (see also, Ben-Yehuda 1997 and Goode and Ben-Yehuda 1994; Becker 1973).[6]

Knowledge about terrorism is controlled and disseminated by experts on the subject. That these experts produce special ways of knowing an object of study is, as Foucault (1979) would argue, a practice of power. It is also evidence of the increase in a practice (the production of expert knowledge and expert discourse) that emphasizes the special language of experts over direct experience. Yet a viable alternative is to study violence with a reexamination of the constructs, conceptualizations, definitions, and discourse used to give meaning to practices of violence, domination, and ter-rorism. Especially in the area of terrorism, where it appears that our knowledge and use of this construct does not differ consider-ably from its use in eighteenth- and nineteenth-century discourse on social reality, a reexamination of relevant contemporary social referents with the production of discourse is needed.

The construct of terrorism, therefore, inherits its meaning from a world in which ideas of democracy, expansion of terri-tory, or colonialism and the expansion of the state as the site of legitimate violence are gaining momentum. The old monarchi-cal regimes and class structures are dying and terrorism is called upon to provoke public fear of change and appeal to its desire for the security of stability. In the contemporary world, relations among the state, economy, and society are continually being threatened. Specifically, the growth of the global economy (especially since the collapse of Soviet-style socialism) juxtaposed with the loss of social meaning regarding the nation-state at the local level, once again challenges longstanding anthropological, ideological, and epistemological assumptions (compare with Frank 1993; Frank and Gills 1993; Kirby 1993). As the nation-state is structurally deconstructed and reconstructed as a result of these global and local forces, the construct of terrorism, representing the height of the nation-state in its formation and politics, is invoked.

Terrorism and Chronopolitics

As the state enters a new phase in its evolution, referents from the past, including the conception of terrorism, are employed. At the local level, cultural, regional, and ethnic struggles are destroying old conceptions and political boundaries at accelerated rates, while the global economy reminds the world of its ultimate interdependence. Even the threat of nuclear holocaust has diminished in recent years. Old nation-states are dismantled and global awarenesses via the new electronic age have set the stage for the development of new social and political relations, nationally and internationally. Alongside such rapid change, however, are more elusive changes which are inexplicable via traditional, paradigmatic forms of knowledge. These changes include the nature of space to place and time to pace.

In a mass-mediated, consumer oriented society, such as the United States or Italy, social, economic, and moral-political life is informed by an endless procession of images. Thus, the power of language and discourse become evidenced increasingly through the exchange of signs and elusive practices rather than material, concrete goods. Thus, discursive practices become an integral, indispensable part of political practice and the practices of power (Nash 1994; Namaste 1993; Virilio 1986; Baudrillard 1983a; deLauretis 1985; Foucault 1979; Gramsci 1966). Der Derian (1990, 297) explicates contemporary practices including chronopolitics (the privileging of "pace" over "space" in international relations) and technostrategics (practices that "use and are used by technology for the purpose of war"), in international relations; he suggests that traditional approaches to research are either inadequate or resistant to understanding these pervasive and elusive practices of states, while discursive analyses are more sensitive to issues of context, style, and political attitudes in order to understand these critical new forces in international arenas. Der Derian (1990, 297) notes:

> These (post)modern practices are elusive because they are more "real" in time than space, their power is evidenced through the exchange of signs not goods, and their effects are transparent and pervasive rather than material and discrete. They do not fit and therefore they elude the traditional and the re-formed delimitations of the international relations field: the geopolitics of realism, the structural political economy of neorealism, the possessive institutionalism of neoliberalism.

This form of critical analysis does not claim to overcome all the inadequacies of other theoretical perspectives or to be uniformly superior to traditional attitudes toward research. It allows for the investigation of processes in contemporary social, political, and economic life that are often suppressed, overlooked, or threatening to those foundations or categories of meaning that claim to be real and representative of reality. Furthermore, the discursive argument defies the idea of binary opposition, theories of estrangement, and definitive concepts and categories as it attempts to analyze not what or why certain structures, forms, or processes exist in society, but rather *how*, by what means or strategies certain structures, forms, and processes are sustained, transformed, or suppressed. In commenting on research in the area of epidemic disease and the American Indian experience, for example, Thornton (1987, xviii) similarly notes:

> Scholars are a cautious group, typically reluctant to go beyond what can be known for certain. The availability of

complete, orderly, and certain information often deter-
mines which topics they choose to study and the ways they
approach selected topics. As a result, many important
issues are unstudied or studied from limited perspectives.

With respect to the present inquiry into the discourse of terrorism in Italy and the United States, the significance of a critical analysis becomes clear. The political power contained in the
discourse of terrorism, and the strategies used to perpetuate it,
shapes knowledge or meaning from historically transient events
such as the *Achille Lauro* or the TWA incidents and re-produces
individuals (citizens) and nation-states as well as the relations
among them. Terrorism is a construct that is best understood as
a relative rhetoric of the state, intrinsic to statecraft.

While the power of "elusive (post)modern practices" becomes
more "real" in time, since the exchange of signs is not readily
apparent when they are occurring (also see Gramsci 1966, 99–119),
we also need to explore the exchange of signs in space in order to
understand the significance of the construction of political realities
that might be viewed as different or in competition with the social,
political, and economic features of the society. The conditions
under which the discourse of terrorism produces notions of identity in society, such as nationalism, sovereignty, ethnicity, culture,
and social order, must be analyzed in different sites or locations
(compare with Anderson 1983). In this way we can attempt to
examine reality in terms of "specific location" or "place" rather
than privileging experiential interpretations: "space generates
time, but time has little relationship to space" (Deloria 1992, 71).

Providing a spatial analysis for the construction of terrorism allows for a more systematic examination of how differ-
ence(s) or deviant identities such as terrorism acquire meaning
via competing interpretations, whether those differences are
defined as economic, social, cultural, or political, and/or at
national or international levels. And, in examining the production of difference, questions involving ideology, knowledge, and
communication and functional questions of an anthropological
sort bearing on humans' and societies' elemental order or being
are intrinsic to a critical analysis.

An observation by Erikson (1966, 12) regarding the emergence of the media and the demarcation of moral boundaries in society serves as a useful point of departure for the study of the discourse of terrorism. The changes he observes as a result of his historical, social analysis of deviance foreshadows research in this area:

> Today of course, we no longer parade deviants in the town square or expose them to the carnival atmosphere of a Tyburn, but it is interesting that the "reform" which brought about this change in penal practice coincides almost exactly with the development of newspapers as a medium of mass information. Perhaps this is no more than an accident of history, but it is nonetheless true that newspapers (and now radio and television) offer much the same kind of entertainment as public hangings or a Sunday visit to the local gaol. A considerable portion of what we call "news" is devoted to reports about deviant behavior and its consequences, and it is no simple matter to explain why these items should be considered newsworthy or why they should command the extraordinary attention they do . . . *they constitute one of our main sources of information about the normative outlines of society.* In a figurative sense at least, morality and immorality meet at the public scaffold, and it is during this meeting that the line between them is drawn. (*emphasis mine*)

In a figurative sense, Erikson presents the mass media as a stage for the presentation and punishment of what becomes defined as "deviant" behavior. His observation about the emergence of the mass media as coinciding with the end of public torture and hangings in the town square is suggestive not only about those who do the brutalizing (whether through their texts or the gaol), but also about those who spectate and speculate about it (compare with Manning 1989; Foucault 1979). It suggests that "deviance" is a social definition that is created, maintained, and transformed through political processes (compare with Lauderdale and Cruit 1993; Farrell and Case 1995).

Erikson notes how the definition and identification of "deviance" is socially and politically important to the creation of moral boundaries by which moral being is differentiated and empowered; in this study a similar association between the definition and identification of terrorism, the production of hegemony, and the construction of political (domestic and international) boundaries by which sovereign political being is constituted as the modern state's ground, source of legitimacy, and basis of power is suggested. These two perspectives, the media as a stage, a stage of and for theater, for the unfolding of the spectacle (or text), and the political reality it suggests, constitute the theoretical and analytical orientation for the study of terrorism as a discursive practice of statecraft unfolding in two relevant sites of struggle, in chronopolitical place and pace.

3

SETTING THE STAGE:
FOUNDATIONS OF MEANING FOR TERRORISM

Consider the following two passages:

In a nutshell, international "incidents" are like a Pirandello play, with each actor giving his or her version of the facts and the spectator quite powerless to judge which version is closest to the truth. Furthermore, the *dramatis personae* often squabble and disagree over the rules of behavior that apply, what exactly these rules say, how they should be interpreted, and even whether they apply at all.

One reason terrorist incidents are so heavily scripted is that both sides like being able to predict, within reason, what will happen. It is when such predictability is not possible that disasters occur.

Each passage contains the metaphor of the *theater* suggesting a particular perspective about events defined as terrorist, such as the *Achille Lauro* and TWA incidents. In each case, a different aspect of the event's development (or plot development) is underscored, re-presenting a particular attitude toward events defined as terrorist. While the first passage highlights an event development characteristic of a Pirandello play, the second highlights the view of theater as embodying a singular form, that of "heavy scripts," implying a singularity of event development, one that is "predictable." In the first passage, the author goes no further than to use the word "incident" to signify the ambiguity and indecisiveness with which the action in the plots may be defined. On the contrary, in the second text, the author is decisive about what the action is, that of "terrorism," and about what genre is most appropriate for the development of that action.

Both texts are characteristic of the rhetorical content, methodology, and ideological context of two different sites for the discourse of terrorism. The first excerpt is written by an Italian lawyer, Antonio Cassese (1989), and the second by Jeffrey Z. Rubin (1986), a professor of psychology in the Program on Negotiation, Harvard Law School. While both texts appear to simply offer a context for the description and explanation of events, each is in the process of shaping a dominant perspective regarding terrorism and its dimensions. These perspectives are informed by their immediate ideological context (that is, the author's perspective, for what purpose or place the manuscript is written, funding for the work), as well as the cultural and social context of their respective societies. In this chapter, specific cultural and social antecedents in Italy and the United States are examined as they have been considered to alter the interpretation of the theater as a medium by which to disseminate knowledge, in this case knowledge about terrorism.

Theater as a Foundation of Meaning in Italy

In attempting to explain "why" Italians behave the way they do politically, many researchers have attempted to ground Italian behaviors, diverse ideologies, and appreciation for multiple and competing interpretations in certain historical, cultural, and social conditions (see, for example, Banfield 1960; LaPalombara 1965; Lumley and Schlesinger 1982; Romano 1984; Pisano 1987; Chubb 1989; McCarthy 1995; Grundle and Parker 1996). And certain dominant interpretations of Italian culture and history are considered to provide important insights on the development of various art forms such as the theater. In examining the nature of the theater metaphor to define or construct terrorist incidents, the social development of the theater itself.

Despite periods in Italian history in which both the rhetoric and collective ambitions of the people expressed the need for national pride and unity exemplified by a uniform, nationalized language, such as during the Risorgimento (1860) or the Fascist era (1920–1943), for the most part, Italians believe that moral and national issues are not necessarily connected. These issues, therefore, cannot be represented in a uniform way. As a nation-state, Italians prefer to be able to express their various opinions, interpretations, and individual interests while "camping on the same territory, held together by habit and utilitarian motives," rather than out of a sense of national fervor (Romano 1984, 25; see also Drake 1989; Di Palma 1977). Romano (1984, 25) writes that "Italians came to think that Italy could exist without being national, that a national pride, far from being necessary could damage its survival, development, and prosperity." Even with the recent political struggle in Italy among the "new and improved" fascist nationalists and the numerous other political parties, a clear distrust of national chauvinism exists (McCarthy 1995; Grundle and Parker 1996). Beyond the basic promises of returning "order" to the present chaotic bureaucracy and exposing various forms of organized crime, Italian nationalists are unable to influence their agenda in the same way they did after World War I. As a result, these groups often resort to violent or corrupt political means, exposing a different meaning for their official rhetoric. Italian citizens end up distrusting words such as "order," interpreting it as an excuse for repression and suppression of diversity. Despite periods of protest by groups such as fascists, most Italians value the diversity of their culture (see Hofmann 1990). Indeed, Romano (1984, 25) notes that after Mussolini's defeat:

> Italians relinquished all desire to be a truly national community, inspired by great collective ambitions and a higher solidarity. . . . Italians were once again united and yet divided against themselves, candidly shrewd and innocently cynical, according to the only existential lesson that they had fully learned from their history.

The history of the Italian peninsula is one of many conquests and colonizations. The various regions have been conquered and reconquered by numerous societies since prehistory

(Drake 1989; Nanetti 1988). With each of the different conquests, cultural aspects such as language changed dramatically, as some remained and others evolved or emerged. The Southern regional tongues, for example, linguistically resemble languages such as Spanish, Greek, Albanian, and Arabic, while in the Northern regions Slavic, French, German, and Hungarian likenesses may be found (Ducibella 1969). Each region has its characteristic "dialect" or native language and each town has variations of the dialect. These different languages are referred to as *dialetti* in Italian. The term *dialetto* or "dialect," however, must be considered carefully within this context. Dialects typically refer to a form of the "standard" language, as though the standard language preceded the dialect and the dialect was a debased or vulgarized version of the "true" language; in the case of Italy, all the dialects preceded what was later identified as the official, state language. What later became defined as *dialetti* or dialects are actually various culturally unique languages. Even the present form of standard Italian is a derivative of the Florentine linguistic dialect, and therefore it embodies the cultural heritage of that particular region of Italy (see Gramsci 1966). Among the regions, different languages or dialects are not necessarily known or comprehended, because they are etymologically different—like walking into a dramatically different country. When speaking in their native tongues, Sicilians and Barese will not understand each other unless they have learned each others' dialects, even though both regions are located in the south (Ducibella 1969).

One of the most obvious problems with discourse on television, radio, and especially newspapers, magazines, journals, and books, is the predominant language form, publicly presented and considered to be the "standard" form of the Italian language. Although one language was chosen by the state (and/or cultural elite of the period) as the national tongue, the one from the Florentine region, it was clearly imposed in the attempt to unify a society composed of many different cultural groups. Gramsci (1966, 199) wrote extensively on language standardization, its ideological and political dimensions, during a time when language standardization was officially most rigidly enforced in a society where a large majority spoke in their own native tongue and were consequently officially declared "illiterate" (see Ramirez and Boli 1987).[1] In *Letteratura e Vita Nazionale*, Gramsci (1966, 199) wrote that "in written form, normative language always presupposes a certain chosen or cultural 'address' and therefore it is always a political, cultural national act" (translation mine).[2] Although most Italians today speak the standardized version of the language, regional dialects and the cultures from which these dialects derive are also maintained. With each different dialect comes a different political, historical, and cultural heritage, and therefore variations in the mode of interpretation are inevitable (Nanetti 1988; Drake 1989; Wagner-Pacifici 1986).

In a country where cultural diversity is usually encouraged, indeed because attempts to create a unified culture failed, media texts will undoubtedly support and further represent these ideas. The interpretation of an incident such as the *Achille Lauro* affair as an act of terrorism, for example, would require using standardized Italian, the language of the state. The dialects, as they reflect ancient forms of different languages, do not have a word to express the concept of terrorism as society has come to know and understand it.

Thus, multiple and competing interpretations, plots, ideas, or stories are constructed and publicly valued, as the Pirandello metaphor by Cassese informs us. Also, his depiction of the "spectator" as "quite powerless to judge which version is closest to the truth" emphasizes a public understanding of the political nature of the interpretations offered. Lenzi (1981, 85), an Italian reporter for *Il Giornale*, has stated that:

> One of the frequent reproaches against the Italian media, particularly by American journalists, is that of almost never separating the news from the comment (about the news). This can be explained historically. . . .

He goes on to explain that the emergence of the media or the press was as an expression of power and as an instrument of political belief. Consequently, newspapers and magazines are for the most part considered to represent the viewpoint of the state or the "official" views and are not considered to contain "the facts" (Ericson, Baranek, and Chan 1987 1989, and 1991). This attitude can partly be attributed to the strict regulation of the press during the Fascist era, as well as the predominance of regional identities (Drake 1989; Hofmann 1990). Officializations or standardizations have historically been viewed by the public as suspect. The media not only speak in standardized Italian, but also their interpretation of an event is in support of a particular political viewpoint, which generally coincides with the ideas and objectives of a particular political party. Thus, the plurality of interpretations reflects and further reifies the diversity of regional cultural identities as well as the political and ideological preferences characteristic of each region. A quote by Aldo Moro (1974), one of the high-ranking officials of the Christian Democratic party during the seventies, declares the following concerning this social diversity in Italy: "This disorganized and discordant Italy is, however, infinitely more rich and alive than the more or less well ordered Italy of the past."[3] Attempts in Italy's past to create political "order" were accompanied by the repression of numerous regional cultures, a sacrifice most Italians hope never to repeat (Forgacs 1986).

The use of the Pirandello metaphor in describing international incidents also assumes a certain sophisticated understanding of the theater. While Cassese's book will undoubtedly attract a limited readership—a readership who will know what Pirandello theater means and may therefore be considered to be an elite audience by American standards—the amusements of the stage have, in fact, been readily available for Italians throughout most of its political history.[4] And throughout much of its political history, the theatrical genre that has often dominated in the representation of political events has been farce or comedy (see Galli 1976; Bechelloni 1984; Wagner-Pacifici 1986). The theater in Italy is not an activity of only the privileged classes. As Tocqueville (1862) noted, the theater provides "multitudes" with "literary gratification," and Italians of all classes have participated in the theater (whether in large-scale productions or at a community *festa* or celebration), regardless of their literary abilities or social-cultural standing.

While the foregoing explanations of and research into historical, social, and cultural contexts provide certain interesting insights concerning "why" certain beliefs or processes may exist in Italy, in this discursive analysis the latter can only be viewed as tangential conjecture. The explanations for the most part still rely primarily on the creation of binary oppositions and historical revisionisms (White 1973) and do little to increase our understanding of the discrete political practices of modern society that allow for the propagation, transformation, or suppression of certain processes and ideas (Der Derian 1990).

While the metaphor of the theater and theater genre is clearly demonstrated in the construction of incidents such as the *Achille Lauro* affair, in Italy "theater" refers to the array of interpretations and discourse generated as a result of such an incident, in the wake of having to define and control it. The theater metaphor itself is conceptualized and abstracted to represent the *processes* whereby political institutions attempt to define the incident. The following section examines this use of the theater metaphor as representing Italian political process with respect to the *Achille Lauro* incident.

The Theater of Terrorism in Italy

In the first text, by Cassese (1989), Pirandello theater is used as a metaphor to characterize the way in which "terrorist" incidents such as the *Achille Lauro* affair are constructed officially by the international community. Briefly, Pirandello theater is characterized by an impromptu dramatic dialogue rather than dialogue based on an already existing narrative. The author does not attempt to establish authority by directing and guiding the action of the characters and the plot of the play—it is the characters who shape and guide the outcome of the production. This metaphor is suggestive of the multiple, often competing interpretations of events aired by the various protagonists of a "terrorist" incident: the state and/or national representatives involved, the people involved in the incident itself, and the media, who are viewed as representing the public's access to the event.

Cassese also metaphorically reiterates a perspective Italians more generally share about the politics of officials or government agencies as grounded in endless dialogue, massive bureaucratic slowdowns, and philosophical disorganization (LaPalombara 1965). The politics of the media are understood within a context of open political partisanship; thus, interpretations of events such as the *Achille Lauro* affair can represent multiple possible realities, none of which are publicly viewed as pure and untransformed (see for example the Aldo Moro incident and media involvement, Drake 1995 and Wagner-Pacifici 1986; Romano 1984; Di Palma 1977; Galli 1974). Certain realities, however, may dominate during a particular historical period (or even for a particular event), and others may be abandoned and perhaps later resuscitated for another time albeit in a different form (Grundle and Parker 1996; Pisano 1987; Lumley and Schlesinger 1982; cf. Lyttleton 1973). Because neither the media nor government officials are viewed as being able to represent a politically "neutral" reality, their discourse foregrounds and calls attention to its subjectivity. Because of this open subjective, partisan context, the public is not misled into believing that official decision making is inspired by a higher moral code embodied in the state or government. On the contrary, because officializations are typically mistrusted by the larger public, the credibility of the government and the media can only be enhanced if they portray themselves as bearers of a perspective (even though it may be the dominating perspective) rather than of truth. In this sense, the production of "truth" is not viewed as separate or standing above the production of politics and power (Foucault 1979).

This apparent blurring of categories between what the state and the media are supposed to symbolize to the public and what they apparently do symbolize can be evidenced in the rhetorical practices of media texts in constructing the plot of an incident such as the *Achille Lauro* affair. The decisions and actions of the Italian government to refrain from using force and to refuse surrendering the Palestinian individuals despite U.S. pressure are at once criticized and applauded by various competing Italian officials. The media reflecting these varied political party viewpoints applauded the Italian government's decision by saying that it demonstrated strength of character in the face of a critical international ally, yet also criticized it for potentially offending a superpower. De Rosa (1987), for example, the captain of the *Achille Lauro*, wrote an article entitled "Una Crise di Governo Imprevista" (An unforseen crisis of government). The title suggests an ironic double meaning. That is, while it is typical for the Italian government to be *in crise* (in a state of crisis), the *Achille Lauro* incident introduced an unexpected crisis (or unpredicted crisis). The "crisis" De Rosa refers to in his article involves the Italian government's response to U.S. pressure. He uses such metaphors as the government's "merrily passing financial laws" (383) and the parliament's "playing with vital national interests" (391), to depict the government's usual political practices, when it is suddenly struck by a crisis that could undermine or potentially threaten "all their creations." The routine national practices of the government are discussed within a farcical context, which appears to clearly undermine the government's authority. By the end of the article, however, he notes that despite this farcical context, the state is keen on maintaining its power and authority; when it is threatened, it rises to the challenge. Such was the case during the *Achille Lauro* incident. The Italian state perceived U.S. pressure as a threat to its political survival, both nationally and internationally. De Rosa (1987), therefore, ends with this resolution: that while defining the government as being in a state of crisis was not an error in the immediate sense, since it indeed collapsed (as it always does) as a result of competing perspectives, defining it as a crisis of state was an error. The state emerged strengthened, renewed, and re-elected. Despite the Italian government's refusal to act according to the desires of its political ally, the United States, it was after all "the decision of a sovereign nation with particular local interests which it must defend and promote" (391). Italians are able to maintain their paradoxical "love-hate" relationship with the United States. At the level of the global economy, the Italian state recognizes its heavy dependence on the United States. However, at the local level, resistance to U.S. cultural encroachment and political domination pervades the society.

Speculation and conjecture within the context of historical and cultural interpretations attempting to explain "why" information is presented and absorbed in a particular way in the United States also proliferate (Shultz and Schmauder 1994; cf. Deloria 1992). A brief overview of some of these interpretations may be useful, not so much for their utility in explaining these processes, but rather for examining their limited, tangential qualities.

Theater as a Foundation of Meaning in the United States

It has been suggested that the dominant way in which information and knowledge is presented in the United States has much to do with certain characteristics inherited by the early European colonizers (McLoughlin 1978; Cherry 1971; Tocqueville 1862). Indeed, despite the rich diversity comprising the United States, dominant conceptions of reality and standards descending from the early colonizers are presented as a monolith. The Puritans who came to the New World in the 1600s abhorred anything to do with entertainment. The theater was considered to be an unnecessary, even evil diversion, causing people to stray from the path of religious righteousness (see McLoughlin 1978; Boyer and Nissenbaum 1974; Cherry 1971; Bentley 1968). Within the last century, the attitude toward theater and drama changed, of course, as did political reforms for various cultures; but for the most part, Americans who indulge in this sort of entertainment are still considered to be from more privileged classes.

The concept of theater does not refer to all forms of stylized action or entertainment, regardless of their cultural or class origin. It refers to a particular type of art, or "culture" as though art or culture were intrinsically separate from the realm of the everyday and could be accessed only in exclusive ways. Theater is viewed as an exclusive form of "high" art, symbolized by Broadway, the site of the most powerful theater. It is not viewed as an inclusive art of the people of which Broadway is an example.

Tocqueville (1862, 484) wrote in the mid-1800s, "People who spend every day in the week making money, and the Sunday in going to church, have nothing to invite the Muse of Comedy." The extreme regularity of habits and the strictness of manners, in his opinion, provided a major obstacle to the growth of everyday forms of art. Yet he also notes that such behavior appeared to be in contradiction to American *laws*, which allowed for the utmost freedom, and even license of language. Instead, the laws were surrendered to the *interpretations* of the "ruling passions." Drama and theater were subjected to censorship and could not take place without the approval of municipal authorities. Whereas in Italy moral and national issues are not necessarily viewed as connected, in the United States they are virtually inseparable. The Constitution, for example, a document representing the political ideals of the American Republic, also presents these ideals within a Christian-moral context. Morality, therefore provides the basis for interpreting dominant, foundational political practices (Demerath and Hammond 1969; Herberg 1955).

Tocqueville's observation about the relative novelty of dramatic art in representing societal conditions in the United States and the strictness with which such art was created and enjoyed has influenced the growth of, and experience with, aestheticized politics in a different way than in Italy (see Wagner-Pacifici 1986; White 1987). Restrictions on artistic expression, literary style, and the choice and treatment of subjects, based on puritan political morality, influenced the development of dramatic representation. Dramatic art was subjected to the same rules and the same laws as the rest of society and these rules were to be respected rather than questioned (Tocqueville 1862). The tendencies of the theater, which were to exaggerate, transgress the rules, or abandon them altogether, were controlled with a strictness of manner characteristic of the Puritan society at the time. Such restrictiveness led to a certain uniformity of interpretation of the theater, despite dissident attempts by later playwrights such as O'Neill or Williams (long after Tocqueville's time) to transcend the boundaries ingrained within the society (Allison *et al.* 1974).

This influence of restrictiveness ultimately influenced the structure of the theater, and the nature of plot development more than content. While the subjects of plays (as well as movies) are often politically and morally daring or challenging to hegemonic assumptions, the structure of their presentation follows conventional narrative modes (Barthes 1977; Artaud 1958).[5] Popular productions that abandon a linear chronological structure are fairly recent and are often defined as "postmodern," e.g., recent movies such as *Pulp Fiction*. However, such modes of representing drama in the theater are not new in the United States (Bentley 1968) (especially among diverse cultural groups), although they have not been accepted or understood by popular culture until recently.

At the same time that laws protecting freedom of expression were being established, the dominant, puritan way of life was affecting the interpretation of those laws (see Stout 1982; Lang 1981; McLoughlin 1978; Erikson 1966). Contemporary examples of this paradox, which encourages freedom of expression but limits freedom of art, can be found in the controversies surrounding such targets of censorship as Calvin Klein and Benetton advertisements, flag art, rap music videos, and television and movie ratings. In addition to the censoring of art which is considered to be too obscene, sexual, or violent, art deprecating dominant U.S. political viewpoints is also either suppressed or marginalized. Museum exhibits re-presenting African American or American Indian art, for example, are currently very popular in the United States; yet rather than depicting the stories of these cultures as told by them, these museums overwhelmingly represent these cultures and peoples as objects of art, not as the subjects and authors of reality, art being an intrinsic part of that reality (Goldberg 1993).[6] In this way, the dominant culture looks upon, observes and examines such depictions from a distance. It is no wonder then that there is no museum of slavery or American Indian holocaust in the United States. Other art forms, such as films and theater, that attempt to represent competing cultural interpretations of history have only recently gained notoriety, e.g., *Dances with Wolves* or *Malcolm X*. However, the notoriety of the latter movies was based more on their innovative technological effects, cinematography, and spectacular marketing techniques than on their interpretation of subject matter (compare with Lauderdale 1995; Deloria 1992).

Just as the dominant interpretation of U.S. history has been presented as a monolith, the theater as art form has been presented in a similar fashion. Multiple interpretations of history at the artistic whim of the producer or author are considered to be potentially threatening to hegemonic facades and representations. Thus, the expressive nature of the stage in the United States, in general, has been transformed to reflect social orders and realities. Productions attempting to represent alternative realities have been either defined as deviant, or have neither been respected nor understood as serious challenges to the state.

To be sure, the United States has experienced certain major social changes over the course of its history. What has not changed are structural representations of social institutions such as the state. The state, as it is understood in society, still represents a relatively brief hegemony (that of the site of legitimate violence) which is thought of as traditional and natural. But the state as it is experienced in contemporary society, as more than just the site of legitimate violence, is still unrepresented and misunderstood (Kirby 1994). Depictions of terrorism, especially as aestheticized politics, reify this outmoded construction of the state. Terrorism, with its surrounding discourse, therefore is more appropriately represented as a form of statecraft and state-production, wherein the state represents itself as the legitimate sovereign, the legitimate site of social control, rather than as a form of domination in everyday life.[7]

Contemporary American theater, furthermore, has developed a certain keen aesthetic skill, or rather a model of realist interpretation based on the reification of binary oppositions, as an attempt to control the political nature of the theater. Interpretations of reality can therefore be convincingly portrayed as singular truths (for example, see Allison 1974 on *The Importance of Being Earnest*). This uniformity of interpretation in the United States has maintained a certain dominance in all discursive forms, whether written or spoken (see Nash 1994; Brown and Merrill 1993; Minson 1985; Pudaloff 1985; Stout 1982; Lang 1981). And rather than viewing this sort of uniformity as limiting or authoritative, it was and is viewed as reflecting order and stability (Pudaloff 1985; Stout 1982; Leverenz 1980). Italian drama, for example, is often looked upon by North Americans as artfully confusing compared to U.S. dramatic productions, which follow a more chronological, linear structural development (White 1987; Simonson 1968).

Thus, the theater metaphor is represented quite differently for the discourse of terrorism in the United States. The theater is conceptualized and abstracted to define the plot of the *actual* incident and the people involved in the incident, rather than representing a political process in action as it did in Italy. The texts by psychology professor Jeffrey Rubin (1986), however, and other writers in the United States who have used and are used by the metaphor of the theater in constructing and defining terrorist events, reflect a different process in the development of a discourse of terrorism and the prescriptive, normative implications therein. The next section examines this alternative meaning.

Theater of Terrorism in the United States

As in Italy, U.S. texts about terrorism are written in what is considered to be a "standard" form of the language with "standard" discursive forms and patterns.[8] However, unlike the Italian example, dialect forms of English (as spoken in the United States) are considered to have occurred after the importation of cultures and peoples who were different from the *founding* ancestors. Thus, dialects have been viewed as vulgarized, derivative, impure forms of English, much the way the people who imported them are viewed (Dinnerstein and Reimers 1988). While the Italians privilege multiple interpretations of "reality" considered to be reflective of their diverse cultural heritage prior to linguistic standardizing, Americans attempt to negate the existence of various cultures (especially indigenous cultures) by claiming to integrate them ("melting-pot" ideological metaphor) into one language, culture, identity, and one clearly dominant form of interpretation (see Deloria 1992; Thornton 1987; Allen 1986).

Research on terrorism in the United States is also often

affected by monolithic representations of reality. Indeed, most research relies on dominant paradigmatic explanations of historical or cultural events. And typically those historical interpretations are dominated by the "winners" of history. Alternative views of the United States' history of terrorism exist, but are not part of hegemonic representations.[9] Commager (1985, 76), for example, writes about terrorism as a longstanding traditional form of political practice that may not be justifiable but is understandable since throughout history major countries have employed terrorist tactics. He notes that the U.S. state provides many examples of this political practice:

> Americans, too, must confess their own history of terrorism against those they feared or hated or regarded as "lesser breeds." Thus, the extermination of the Pequot Indians as early as 1637; the Sand Creek massacre of some 500 Cheyenne women and children in 1864—and this after the tribe had surrendered; the lurid atrocities against Filipinos struggling for independence at the beginning of this century; Lieut. William L. Calley's massacre of 450 Vietnamese women, children and old men at Mylai in 1969.

This view of U.S. history stands in sharp contrast to the "discovery of Columbus" view (Stevens 1976).

While events themselves are often credited with producing change, underlying forces contributing to the conditions for change are often overlooked. Ostensible terrorist events are often viewed in this way, as providing the reason for changes in the state's policies (whether internationally or domestically) or to justify the state's action against "other" societies. In 1945, for example, the bombing of Hiroshima and Nagasaki by the United States was carried out after the Japanese had clearly lost the war. This act was (and is) recounted primarily as a preventive measure and rarely as a retaliatory move by the United States for the Japanese "terrorist" attack at Pearl Harbor. But the difference between the two attacks is significant. While the Japanese attack was directed at the military base (even though the base was unprepared for it), the fateful atomic bombing was directed against civilians. Commager (1985) refers to this type of attack as exemplifying the "formal rationalization—we might almost say legitimization—of terrorism [which] came with World War II when all the major participants abandoned 'precision' bombing ... for saturation bombing. ... It was a policy that eventually took the lives of millions of women and children in London, Coventry, Hamburg, Berlin, Dresden, Warsaw, Moscow, Tokyo and scores of other 'open cities.'" For Commager, the practice of saturation bombing was a systematic process whose use might be understood more by understanding the process of formal rationality in society than simply as a retaliatory act (see Weber 1954 and 1958). Indeed, by Vietnam, this practice of bombing civilians was taken for granted and even more systematized as the United States poured "seven million tons of bombs on Vietnam, Cambodia and Laos—three times the tonnage dropped on Germany and Japan during World War II" (Commager 1985, 77). The United States was not technically at war with Vietnam, Cambodia, or Laos, but the practice of terrorism was so "rationalized" at this time that it did not even inspire recognition or definition as "terrorism." (And defining missiles as "smart" in the Gulf War when they explode on civilian targets is further problematic.)

Inverarity *et al.* (1983, 79) provide another type of example of this process whereby events are considered to be the most significant driving force leading to social change, rather than underlying processes. They examine the formulation of civil rights laws and their acceptance in U.S. society. Despite the enactment of the "Civil Rights Act of 1875 granting blacks the right to 'full and equal enjoyment' of all forms of public transportation, entertainment and housing as well as the right to serve on juries," the state did not even begin to honor this law until the end of the second civil rights revolution in the 1960s. Inverarity *et al.* (1983) attribute this change more to underlying economic and political transformations in the society, which facilitated the inclusion of African Americans, than simply to the civil rights protests against discrimination in the 1960s.

Similarly, the increase in social control, surveillance, and security at airports, which is attributed to the need to control terrorism, may in fact be due more to the increase in public dependence on air flight as a form of transportation. But identifying the cause as being terrorism (or, for civil rights legislation, the cause as being protest movements) reifies and facilitates the construction of political boundaries: divisions among people, binary oppositions, or enemies, the idea that Americans need to fear someone.

In order to analyze terrorism, however, as it is currently involved in shaping social views and action, texts on terrorism from Italy and the United States require a different understanding which goes beyond extant conceptions and ideas to how they are transformed. How are they constructed and sustained such that their meaning becomes viewed as fixed, based on reality, and hence certifying them as sources of power? Der Derian (1990, 298) states the problem to be the following:

> The closer . . . scientific discourse bring(s) us to the "other"—that is, the more that the model is congruent with the reality, the image resembles the object, the medium becomes the message—the less we see of ourselves in the other. Back to the big American car: reflection loses out to reification.

With respect to the discourse of terrorism in the United States, the traditional constructions of binary oppositions, fixed in social realities, appear to be more a part of contemporary American dialogue than of Italian dialogue. Terrorism in the United States is presented as drama, as the plot for theater, in order to make us believe that what follows the incident, the interpretations of the incident and the political action taken to neutralize the incident, is not theater, not the unfolding of a drama in itself, but the exercise of justice and truth fixed by facts (Namaste 1993; cf. Baudrillard 1983a). The Italian theater of terrorism focuses on what happens after the incident occurs. Terror and violence are instead viewed as aspects of daily life, and the drama or theater of terrorism represents the processes that occur as a result of the incident: the processes of the media and state that unfold whereby we can define the other, the terrorists, and punish them so that their actions provide the occasion for (but not necessarily the reason for) the punishment. Furthermore, with the help of the media we can broadcast such information and interpretations of reality so that everyone may know who and what "terrorists" are, what happens to them, and what we are to avoid.

Despite the ambiguities suggested in the Italian texts, in the end there is a certain reification of authority by the state; but this occurs more out of a sense of resolve than of commitment. In other words, the theater of terrorism in Italy allows for a greater public recognition of the arbitrary role of the state and the political purpose of interpreting incidents and acts of terror than the theater of terrorism in the United States, which further reifies binary oppositions of good and evil—state as good and persons acting against the state as evil or terrorists. Furthermore, the Italian theater of terrorism appears to go beyond the question of whether or not terrorism is being represented falsely, but rather highlights the unreality (farcical, melodramatic, if you will) of reality in the identification, definition, and recognition of terrorism.

PART II

THE TELLING OF STORIES
ON DIFFERENT STAGES

4

(Re)Constructing the Event:
The *Achille Lauro* Plot

On October 7 1985, an Italian luxury liner named *Achille Lauro* was seized off the coast of Egypt between Alexandria and Port Said. The liner was on its way to Port Said. Between staff members and passengers, there were approximately 500 people aboard. Out of the approximately 300 staff persons, more than 200 were Italian. Out of the estimated 200 passengers, there were about thirty Italian and fifteen U.S. citizens.[1] A group of three Palestinian men on board were responsible for the seizure. In exchange for the safe return of the *Achille Lauro*, the group of three asked for the release of fifty Palestinians held prisoner in Israel. One American was killed.

Beyond a basic chronology of events, it is very difficult to provide a detailed representation of the incident without also constructing it. Deciding what to include and disregard, even for what appears to be an unbiased reporting of facts, is of course an interpretive practice. And so begins my analysis of the (re)construction of events and interpretations of the *Achille Lauro* incident.[2]

Italian Reconstruction

The discourse of terrorism surrounding the *Achille Lauro* incident continually vacillated among understandings and conceptions of reality about the incident itself and the various protagonists of the incident. Italians were attempting to construct order out of the disorder incurred by the crisis by generating multiple and competing interpretations until one interpretation finally dominated. This is how the theater metaphor becomes particularly evident in representing Italian terrorism. It represents the discursive process of arriving at a socially negotiated definition for the incident, including whether or not it would be defined as terrorist. The media provide the stage for the production of different genres representing the same event.

While texts such as Cassese's (1989) use the Pirandello metaphor to represent this process of social negotiation, other texts, such as De Rosa's (1986, 383) (the captain of the *Achille Lauro*), are more decisive about what type of genre best depicts the incident. De Rosa uses a combination of satire and melodrama in his depiction. The title of one of his texts on the incident, for example, is "Una Crisi Di Governo Imprevista," which translates to "An Unpredicted Government Crisis." While the central discussion in the article is serious, the title is satirical and ironic. The government in Italy is always in a state of crisis, especially by U.S. standards (Wagner-Pacifici 1986; Di Palma 1977; Grundle and Parker 1996). Since World War II, there have been more governments than years; government crises are not only predictable but expected (Bobbio 1983; Di Palma 1977). De Rosa (1986) suggests that the Italian government acted appropriately and confidently in the way it managed the incident, especially in the face of other, larger, more internationally powerful actors involved in the crisis, such as Egypt and the United States. Yet, upon the conclusion of what had been perceived as a successful management of the incident, tensions erupted among the different parties comprising Italy's coalition government. The conflict concerned Italy's relationship with its most important ally, the United States, whose policy toward such incidents, especially at this historical moment, was to ostensibly resolve them—by use of force, if necessary (see Lauderdale and Cruit 1993, 187–88). These tensions provided the catalyst for the Italian government's collapse, almost by default.

In Italy, texts such as magazines and, in particular, newspapers overtly display the political position they support. There are approximately fifty legitimate political parties in Italy, and for almost every political party there is a published text or newspaper presenting its ideas. The discrepancies among political positions generate discrepancies among interpretations and competition for the "best" or most politically and contextually acceptable interpretation. The following comment, for example, appeared in a politically liberal newspaper, *Corriere della Sera*. *Corriere* presents the official views of the Italian Christian Democratic Party. In one edition of *Corriere*, the writer attempted to denigrate the viewpoint expressed in another newspaper, *Avanti*, with whom *Corriere* is in competition, presenting the political viewpoint of the Republican party. The passage in *Corriere* not only demonstrates the subjectivity of its perspective, and of the government's perspective, but it does so within a framework characteristic of a dramatic farce (Bentley 1968). Writers Munzi and Stagno (1985, 1) stated that:

> The *Avanti* behaves brutally: it prints inadmissible discourse, which if it was inspired by a minister, responsible for defense, it would be all the more irresponsible and predatory. People asked Spadolini (the Minister of Defense) if he had read the *Avanti* article to whom he responded: I read la *Voce*, also because I write it.

Thus, the discourse of terrorism in Italy surrounding the *Achille Lauro* incident both used and was used by theatrical genre and metaphors to sustain certain political norms about the state, nationality, and international relations, as well as the norms of an Italian perspective of pluralism and/or democracy (Mouffe 1979). At the same time that the government was ridiculed or criticized by various media sources because of its involvement in what was considered to be an international incident, a certain national support was also sustained. And as was apparent in the *Corriere* article, sometimes both these themes were represented in the same article, sometimes even the same passage. The political partisanship of the newspapers, *Corriere*, *Voce*, and *Avanti*, was clearly reflected in both the content of the opinions expressed and the way they were expressed: via direct or open comparisons with each other.

The Italian government was unwilling to utilize force to extradite the Palestinian group to the United States and arrest Abul Abbas (the suspected leader of the group, who was not involved in this incident), as a way of resolving the incident (as per American instructions). Italian government officials were also reluctant to define the incident as an occurrence of "terrorism." The prescriptive implications of Cassese's (1989) text reflect this ambivalence regarding the definition of the incident. Defining the incident as "terrorist" became more a matter of international import favoring the superpower, than of social or national significance in Italy. In other words, the Italian government did not perceive the Palestinians' action as vicariously threatening. First of all, international relations between Italy and Palestine had been mostly favorable; Italy was not about to sacrifice this relationship (De Rosa 1987; Pisano 1987). Second, Italians had learned from their own experiences with the Red Brigades that reacting forcibly often exacerbated the situation. The Red Brigades' action was more effectively subdued *vis-à-vis* discursive competition than by force of arms (see Wagner-Pacifici 1986; della Porta 1995; Drake 1995). Indeed, a violent confrontation between the government and Red Brigades, provoked by their action, was what the Brigades had wanted, especially with the kidnapping of Italian Prime Minister Aldo Moro in 1978. Since then, the rush to define acts as "terrorist" in order to justify a reactionary response by the state has diminished. In recent years, other activities, defined as Mafia, and corporate, corruption by *tangenti* (kickbacks), have replaced terrorism as the "real" threat to the survival of the Italian state (Chubb 1989).[3]

While Italians attempt to approximate some notion that an absolute "truth," regarding terrorism exists, in reality this truth has been decided by a process of discursive competition. Its demarcation or the normative outlines created are admitted to be arbitrary political decisions. This attitude can be deciphered by Cassese's (1989) statement about how the *dramatis personae* squabble and disagree over what the rules are, which ones apply and how they should be interpreted, and even whether they should be used at all. Also, the use of the term "incidents" rather than simply naming the incident further underscores the process by which the incident is constituted, the political nature of its constitution and the arbitrariness of the means chosen to resolve the issue.

This ambivalence was also displayed in Italian press reports representing government decisions. For example, after the occurrence of the incident, Italian magistrates decided the following in the case of the *Achille Lauro*:

> It is true that this politico-military organization [the PLF] possesses all the basic features of an armed band: a number of adherents, and inner hierarchical structure of a military type, possession of arms. But, these features are essential to the organizations' main objective: to help return the Palestinians to their country of origin. These adherents have coalesced around that objective, to achieve it, they created that structure, bought those arms, carried out those actions—of a military, terrorist or political nature—that the Front thought necessary, in diverse situations and according to its ideology and strategic vision of things. There is no evidence that objective ever changed. (Cassese 1989, 118)

The use of the phrase "military, terrorist *or* political in nature" and "armed band" illustrates the magistrates' ambiguity in defining the group as terrorist. Also, the military allusions render terrorism as similar to military practices. Both are involved in politics (sometimes violent), the latter having the advantage of being legitimate (Tilly 1985). This phrase reflects an understanding of terrorism as a form of politics and power, and of its re-presentation in other societal organizations such as the military (Foucault 1979).

Accordingly, the media maintained and supported the decision of the magistrates by publishing articles (in *Corriere* and *Cronaca Contemporanea*, for example) entitled "Were the hijackers terrorists or 'Freedom Fighters'?" and "Was the hijacking of the Italian liner an act of terrorism?" Clearly, despite the general public's skepticism toward the Italian government concerning national issues, support for the state's decision at an international level was another issue. After initial attempts by competing political parties and factions to undermine the part(ies) in power, the discourse focused less on undermining the decision of the government in power and more on establishing its authority in international relations. The following statements by Cassese (1989, 88, 62) echo this view:

> I shall not dwell on how the superpower "bullied" Italy: The Americans behaved in such a way as to violate Italian sovereignty, giving rise to spirited protests from its Mediterranean cousin (Egypt) and a demand for an official apology which, it seems, was never made, at least not in public. A superpower, such as the United States, is not, and never will be, shackled by international rules of behavior or ties of friendship or good diplomatic relations when it has to save defenseless Americans, or punish terrorists who endanger their lives.

Cassese goes on to say that the U.S. use of force (and desire to use more force than necessary) went beyond the immediate situation. Ironically, Cassese turns the definition of terrorism on its ear. One of the main conceptual issues defining events as terrorist involves the violation of a nation-state's sovereignty (Stehr 1994; Schmid and Jongman 1988; Stohl 1988). This fundamental conceptual issue regarding terrorism may be traced to its eighteenth- and nineteenth-century intellectual descendancy. The implication in the above text is that the United States behaved as a terrorist by defying Italian political sovereignty. Also, the metaphor of "cousin," in referring to Egypt as Italy's "Mediterranean cousin," represents the culturally bonded relationship not just between Italy and Egypt, but between Italy and the Northern African countries around the Mediterranean area. The reification of this relationship is of significance because it transcends artificially imposed territorial political boundaries and military alliances.

Another interesting interpretation suggested in the text concerns the reactionary response to acts defined as "deviant," in this case as "terrorist." Cassese suggests that the use of force by the United States served as a warning to the whole world not to challenge the superpower. In other words, the U.S. state reaction was an attempt not only to deter future similar acts, but also to educate the international community and to display its political prowess. The "terrorist" act, therefore, may be viewed as the occasion for but not necessarily the reason for reactionary measures. In this light, despite the state emphasis on eliminating such action by reacting forcibly to it and thereby punishing those who challenge its authority, the actual response or levying of punishment is not done for the sake of the offender, but for political purposes (compare with Inverarity *et al.* 1983; Foucault 1979; Girard 1977; Durkheim 1948). We need only to refer to the analogy of a similar situation at the national level in the United States: the expansion of criminal law and punitive sanctions, which has led to an increase in prison populations—not the opposite. The use of violence to control terrorism is viewed as a socially acceptable state response to the act. Yet, as the past teaches us, most deviants inclined to terrorist action either may long to be or are martyred for their cause, not just for religious reasons but also for political reasons of exposing the hypocrisy of the state. This suggestion is reminiscent of Durkheim's theoretical point regarding the relationship between crime and punishment, that is, that punishment is more proactive than reactive (Inverarity *et al.* 1986, 128–9). "Terrorism" becomes a scapegoat for a much larger struggle surrounding the United States and provoking such a response (see Erikson 1966).

Cassese finally comes around to using the word "terrorism" in his identification of the *Achille Lauro* seizure. With the exception of the book's title, *Terrorism, Politics and Law*, however, the term terrorism does not appear in the body of the book until two-thirds of the way along and only after a chapter entitled "The Italian Judges' Verdict." Through his location and use of the term terrorism, he distances himself and his own ideological position. Terrorism becomes a sign or code representing the ideas of the state, as though the discourse of "terrorism" is a part of the discourse of state, national, and international politics, not of the public at large. Throughout the rest of the book he attempts to maintain the term within this realm. He uses other words such as incident, event, and ordeal as a way of clearly distancing himself from the official opinion. In this way Cassese not only suggests that the term "terrorism" emerged as a result of the judges' verdict or the official, state *interpretation* of events, but he also legitimates his own ambivalent, perhaps separate, estranged position.

Another inherent assumption in the ambivalence of the Italian state to define the *Achille Lauro* incident as a definite case of "terrorism" is the idea that all ethnic groups have the right to establish themselves as sovereign entities; groups and organizations struggling for this cause are not considered to be illegitimate. Even if the organization fights against a foreign country, as long as it is not considered to be directly attacking the interests of the foreign country (in this case, Italy), with which it is not in conflict historically, territorially, and culturally, such action is not considered to be subversive. Consider the following passage from *Corriere della Sera* by Francesco Alberoni (1985, 1)

L'uomo della strada in America non capisce perche mai Paesi come l'Italia, la Jugoslavia o l'Egitto si permettano di impedire al loro soldati di prendere dei delinquenti, ed anzi li proteggano, diano loro del salvacondotti. Dopo quarat'anni in America no ha piu una idea chiara di che cosa possa voler dire sovranita nazionale. Per lui L'America e tutto, i Paesi amici devono ubbidire. Le forze armate americane sono le uniche forze armate legittime. L'ordine che viene da Washington deve essere eseguito. Punto e basta.

The typical person off the street in the United States does not understand why countries like Italy, Yugoslavia, or Egypt permit impeding the military (or police) from arresting delinquents, and instead protect them. After forty years in the United States, one no longer has a clear view of what "sovereignty" can mean. The American military is considered to be the only legitimate armed force. Orders from Washington must be followed. Period, enough.

The article by Alberoni was written in December, rather than in October when the incident occurred. The significance of when the article was written, for the discourse and theater of terrorism, is that most of the competing opinions and viewpoints that could have posed a threat to the government were, for the most part, generated in the first week of the crisis. By December, the viewpoint in support of not only the government but apparently also Italian nationality and ethnic sovereignty predominated.

While the event (re)constructions in a text are significant to the development of a plot for the terrorist drama, because of how it relays information, characterization gives the drama life. Characterization is a primary means by which the audience, spectator, or reader of a text is made to identify with or distance themselves from other persons, whether individuals, groups, or nationalities (compare with Sharif 1996). It is a key component in the creation of the "other" or the "deviant." The characters in a play will draw us in (or repel us) in a variety of ways: through empathy, laughter, indignation, or apathy. Thus, the next section concerns itself with characterization, one of the most efficient ways to construct the other, the evil—in this case, the terrorist.

Characterization

One of the most significant aspects of a stage or theater production is the actors and their characters. Aristotelian poetics and theater were more concerned with the *action* of the character, while the notion of the character as a fully constituted being with a psychological consistency was epitomized in the bourgeois novel (compare, for example, Bremond and Todorov, in Barthes 1977). The development of the actors or characters is significant to the development of the plot. Depending upon whether the production is a comedy, tragedy, or melodrama, characterization is viewed as one of the most important distinguishing features of genre (Wagner-Pacifici 1986; Ferrarotti 1980; Bently 1968; Frye 1957).

The way the characters are brought to life on the stage has the effect of engaging the audience differently; therefore, depending upon whether the author or playwright is interested in emphasizing the action of the plot or deemphasizing it, the characterization will vary. In a melodrama, for example, the characters are depersonalized agents of action or representatives of human characteristics such as gullibility, evil, greed, or goodness, thus emphasizing the action of the plot and deemphasizing the person of the character. If they were to embody a psychological essence the characterizations would be emphasized over the plot, which is more characteristic of tragedy. The audience would be made to identify, ponder, and assess the person of the character as though the character were a real human being, often even before he/she acted.

Texts on terrorism by the media can also emphasize, deemphasize, or simply influence the plot construction depending upon how the protagonists of the incidents are portrayed, if they are portrayed at all (compare with Hugo 1988). Interviews by the media, for example, featuring victims of terrorism and their families or even the terrorists themselves provide an effective forum (or stage) for the development of characters in the terrorist drama. Those who are called the terrorists are rarely (if ever) portrayed as embodying the same needs, desires, characteristics, and possessions as non-terrorists. In contemporary portrayals in the United States of Palestinians, rarely are they shown as having families, or as sharing the same revolutionary spirit of independence and self-determination as the early Americans are portrayed against the British. On the contrary, outbreaks of violence in 1993 and 1995 in the United States that were defined as "terrorist" were immediately assumed by the media and a number of U.S. politicians to have been the work of Palestinians or other Middle Eastern groups. The argument is that such violence is a normal, integral part of their historical and political culture and not typical of U.S. culture.[4] How the actor(s) of an incident are portrayed has a profound impact on perceptions of violent versus non-violent political cultures, in re-presenting both history and contemporary situations, and despite conflicting realities.

The *Achille Lauro* incident offers examples of how the protagonists were displayed in both the U.S. and Italian media. Even though on-the-spot media coverage was more difficult for the *Achille Lauro* incident, numerous texts emerged later. A movie of the week was even made about the incident—or rather the people involved in the incident—allowing viewers supposedly to experience the incident in their own homes. In Italy, media coverage focusing on interviews with the various government and judicial officials involved in the *Achille Lauro* incident outnumbered interviews with the hostages and/or their waiting families at home while the reverse was true in the United States (see Wagner-Pacifici 1986).[5] The following section examines more closely certain salient aspects of characterization, its relationship to genre, the construction of plot, the public's relationship to the characters, and the consequent production of political norms.

Beyond observing that each passage exemplifies how terrorism and terrorists are portrayed in contemporary texts, three more common features are relevant to an analysis of genre formation. To begin with, the characterization of each text clearly reifies a particular political (or ideological) position regarding the practical action that should be used to resolve such situations. Second, they exemplify discursive practices of power. In this sense, power is to be viewed as Foucault (1979) views it, as a positive, productive force that works toward the construction and imposition of a fixed knowledge about terrorism. We are called upon to recognize ourselves and our own behavior as politically normal and appropriate for the production of individual (or national) autonomy compared to the behavior of and identity given to the terrorist other. These texts all work to establish identity, a fixed origin of meaning, and boundaries allowing us to know the difference between "good" and "evil." Third, an implicit claim in the discourse of the following texts is that total knowledge about terrorism and terrorists can be achieved. Reasoning "man" prevails in the end, and through his reason we are able to transcend all ambiguity and all fear associated with ambiguity. Because we have total knowledge, we can feel free to repress that which we have defined as dangerous and evil. This is the same claim that justifies repression and violence by the state and allows the state to conduct "terror" without its actions being defined as "terrorism" (Gibbs 1989).

The texts, although from diverse sources, may be seen as

re-presenting the state, as they all directly echo its promise of political sovereignty, transcendence, knowledge, power, and autonomy, i.e., once we know what and who the deviants (terrorists) are, we can justify our means to eradicate them, or socially control any further similar behavior and achieve freedom/knowledge (compare with Ashley and Walker 1990).

Genre and Characterization

The texts to be analyzed in this section invite a particular response to the acts of the characters in the *Achille Lauro* event. Despite the use of the terms "terrorist" and "terrorism," the hero/villain dichotomy is not as striking in the Italian texts as in the American texts. In the Italian texts, there is a sense of irony that intermingles with the development of the characters, in this case the villains or "terrorists." They are not simply objectifications of evil pitted against the objectification of good; their characters inspire a sense of humanness and comprehensibility. Their relationship to society is highlighted, as is a sense of the supremacy of a "natural law" which overrides the decisions, pronouncements, and presentations of the officials, who ultimately are comprised of the same ambiguities as the "terrorists" themselves. This ambiguity within the characterization of the protagonists is suggested to be a significant feature in the genre of tragedy (Barthes 1977).

Frye (1957, 37–38) has commented on the development of the tragic hero as having "to be of a properly heroic size, but his fall is involved both with a sense of his relation to society and with a sense of the supremacy of natural law, both of which are ironic in reference." Furthermore, the villains are portrayed in the same way as the heroes, allowing for a different relationship between the character and the audience than in a melodrama. Wagner-Pacifici (1986, 286) writes: "For if the protagonists are human, then they are like us and we must identify with some or all of their aspects, heroes and villains alike. And we are forced to ask, What is 'terrorist' within ourselves or what could be terrorist within ourselves, or, finally, how did we create the terrorists?"

In each of the Italian texts, a sense of ambiguity is introduced for the characters of both the hero and the villain. This development of ambiguity is especially striking in the Court of Assize (1986, 2) magistrates' interpretation regarding the action taken by the Palestinians in question:

> Al Assadi, Al Molqi, Fataier were all born in those refugee camps in which the problems besetting the Palestinian people take on violent hues; they grew up—hardly by choice— in an atmosphere of often indiscriminate violence; because of the indifference of others to their problems, they were led to believe that these problems could only be solved by the use of arms. This was the breeding ground for their unfortunate actions: at an age when children usually have other interests, the three men learned to use deadly weapons (both Fataier and Al Molqi joined Palestinian armed organizations at the age of nine; Al Assadi did likewise at eleven . . .

The judges also note that the three men in question had spent their youth in different military units including a "suicide unit." They did not live with their families back at the refugee camps. Not only are the judges acutely aware that their pronouncements, definitions, and decisions are merely what is required by judicial proceedings, but they are attempting to understand the defendants' actions within a social/historical as well as social/psychological context, rather than simply as a short-term, greed-driven desire. The defendants are not simply being blamed. The audience is being asked to identify (so that we may later sympathize or empathize) with the hardships and struggles faced by the defendants, leading to their actions. Also, by providing a political context for the behavior of the defendants, the judges' text invites the notion of terrorism as violence that may be employed by anyone who feels at a disadvantage (whether real or imagined). Violence is contextualized as a part of everyday life—not simply the act of a "terrorist" or of a disenfranchised other who is acting out.

The passage by Alberoni (1985, 1) further expands the development of the "villains" as human beings not by what he says but how he says it:

Pero gli americani avevano ormai adottato la dottrina del-
l'intervento militare, e hanno dirottato l'aereo egiziano con
a bordo i terroristi e Abu Abbas fino a rasentare un conflitto
armato con l'Italia tanto in Sicilia come a Ciampino. L'opin-
ione pubblica americana, d'altra parte, non ha mai perdonato all'Italia di aver lasciato scappare il terrorista Abbas,
cioe di no aver lasciato agire i miliatri della Sesta Flotta.
Non ha mai perdonato all'Italia, ed in particolare a Craxi e
ad Andreotti, di aver dato il primato alla diplomazia
anziche all forza alla punizione. Per gli americani i terroristi di qualunque Paese siano, dovunque agicano, sono dei
criminali comuni che le loro forze armate possono inse-
quire, arrestare, processare.

But the Americans had already adopted the doctrine of military intervention and they had redirected the Egyptian air-
plane carrying the terrorists and Abu(l) Abbas, attempting
to provoke an armed conflict with Italy. On the other side,
American public opinion never forgave Italy, and in particular Craxi and Andreotti for privileging diplomatic means
over force and punishment. For Americans, no matter what
country the terrorists are from, they are all criminals (in
common) which justifies their (American) use of armed
forces, arrest, and prosecution.

Alberoni calls attention to the binary oppositions that exist
for both the government's representations of good and evil and
the public's. In noting the homogeneity of perspective that
exists among the government, media, and public, he is recon-
firming the homogeneity of perspective that exists between his
immediate text and his audience. He contrasts the United States
to Italy, Craxi and Andreotti to Reagan and Shultz, Italian public to American public. In establishing the contrast, Alberoni is
also interpreting the level of ambiguity with which terrorism is
viewed among the Italian public as well as the political means
considered best to manage it.

Another way in which the Italian texts provide for a certain
ambiguity or blurring of categories between what is defined as

terrorist and what may be perceived as terrorist is through the use of personification. The state, the media, the public, and the terrorist for the most part are depicted as machine-like, depersonalized, depoliticized realities, to which one must relate politically, (as a symbolic gesture) without question. The public is expected to accept these entities as definitive, timeless realities. Yet in the Italian text a certain generic slippage occurs when any one of these "entities" is given human features. The language used to represent these features is not characteristic of an abstract machine but of a person. For example, Alberoni uses terms such as "American public opinion never *forgave* Italy," and Cassese uses the term "American *cousin*," rather than ally, and avers that the "superpower *bullied* Italy." The use of personification is paradoxical, of course, for while it attempts to portray non-human entities as human beings in the apparent attempt to bring us closer to the abstractions, it simultaneously makes us realize just how impersonal the "machine" really is or how "unreal" it is. Representing it as having human features accomplishes the opposite—it reifies the machine's absence of feelings, relationships, or behaviors—yet it has ultimate control over our lives. The effect of such a personification, furthermore, allows for a response beyond mere "praise" or "blame" of either the system or the terrorist. By presenting the paradoxes, it allows us to consider them and to respond to them more thoughtfully.

Since World War II, Italy has had more than fifty-one governments. Belief in the democratic process is more than simply a belief. Whether through protest, elections, or the creation of new political parties, Italians actively attempt to sustain the notion of political participation, often at the expense of their domestic stability.[6] Too much stability is suspect, too little (compared to America) at least allows for the free flow of ideas and heterogeneity necessary to a democratic society. The level of ambiguity that slips into the notion of terrorism, therefore, further sustains Italian domestic political interests and reputation for heterogeneity; however, the homogeneity of opinion that can be observed between the media, the public, and the government suggests that the ambiguities introduced in the texts may have been more apparent than real, considering Italian international interests at the time.

When the *Achille Lauro* incident occurred and the government of the Christian Democrat party (DC) firmly declared its conviction to use diplomatic instead of military action, the Republicans were very critical of the decision. Newspapers such as *Avanti* presented the Republican position, while *Corriere della Sera* presented the DC position. The Republicans claimed that by rejecting U.S. demands and allowing intervention by Arafat and the Palestine Liberation Organization (in denouncing terrorist acts), Italy had proclaimed itself as a defender of terrorism and not of international peace. These differences of opinion led to the domestic crisis of government. However, the DC's perspective prevailed in public opinion, especially after the party was reelected. They effectively compared Italian political experiences with some of the political problems faced by Palestinians today as well as Italian national and international interests (Pisano 1987).

Furthermore, the Italian government was able to assert its strength by firmly declining the demands of its allied superpower. This action brought about renewed public faith in the DC despite attempts to discredit their decision. Previously, economic dependence on the United States and constant political fragmentations had kept Italian international politics effectively controlled at the international level. However, their determination not to surrender to American pressure provided a certain national solidarity at the domestic level and respect for the government's resolution of the event at the international level (De Rosa 1987).

The idea of an overriding subjective understanding of reality is also highlighted by the Italian texts and their use of ambiguity in the depiction of the heroes and villains. The texts by the Magistrates of Genoa and by Alberoni establish this through their characterization and blurring of definitions/categories for people and entities. The text by Cassese (1989, 64) establishes this with a more direct questioning of the melodramatic genre:

[A]s Pascal noted—justice changes with latitude and what is true on one side of the Pyrenees is false on the other. A consensus has now formed on a set of rules to regulate relations between states; these rules enshrine values and interests that all states, or almost all, hold dear. In principle, at least, Good and Evil should not vary according to latitude and longitude. It is therefore pertinent to ask whether or not, in a case such as the *Achille Lauro* incident, a superpower has respected these rules and why.

He intimates that an objective understanding of good and evil must exist at least procedurally in international relations, but specifically whether or not these objective values are always applied is another issue. He chooses to question whether the United States has respected these rules, since it is the United States who initiates their establishment but does not necessarily adhere to them should its interests be viewed as jeopardized or threatened. Thus, the superpower's position and interests predominate, and the rules are established to control the interests of the allies—not necessarily the interests of the superpower. Cassese's text is especially pertinent for his suggestive use of the melodramatic genre with respect to political norms and interests. The established norms are sustained as a result of political procedure, not necessarily morality. There is an inherent realization of and distancing from the subjective construction of political norms, interests, and values and their variance over time and space, unlike the timeless construction of political norms, morality, and interests suggested in most American texts on terrorism.

While the Italian texts re-present the process of discursive competition and social negotiation for the definition of the *Achille Lauro* incident, the U.S. texts re-present a different process. The texts begin with the premise that the definition of terrorism has already been established. The texts, therefore, further construct this assumption in their dramatic presentations as well as reify what that definition is—that terrorists personify evil at its worst. We now turn to how this perspective is created, by examining the TWA incident of 1984.

5

(Re)Constructing the Event:
The Hijacking of TWA 847

On June 14, 1985, Trans World Airlines Flight 847, a Boeing 727 jet plane en route from Athens to Rome was hijacked to Beirut by two Lebanese Shiites. There were approximately 145 passengers on board from different nations. For the following two days, the two Lebanese men flew the plane back and forth from Lebanon to Algeria, releasing passengers in each place. One passenger, a U.S. Navy person, was killed. The plane finally landed in Beirut with about forty passengers, including the crew, who were handed over to Amal Nabih Berri, considered to be the mastermind of the group. In exchange for the hostages, Berri wanted the release of 700 Lebanese prisoners taken by Israel in southern Lebanon. The event lasted until June 30, 1985, when the U.S. citizens were released and the Lebanese prisoners were subsequently released by Israel.

In the three and one-half weeks of the event's duration, the TWA story dominated the media—both televised and written. What ensued was a skilled aestheticized scenography of the event that included an airport press conference with the U.S. passengers and the Shiites, three-way interviews on television with Berri, selected passengers, the expectant family members, and interviewer David Hartman. "ABC World News Tonight" and "Good Morning America," as well as *Time*, *Newsweek*, and *U.S. News and World Report* produced and reproduced the event from the moment of its occurrence to its ostensible ending. Like the *Achille Lauro* incident a few months later, numerous mediated narratives were constructed, to appeal to the public's dramatic senses. The media's interpretations were framed, as they usually are, in what appeared to be organized and cohesive stories among the various protagonists, even though the event was anything but organized and cohesive. In other words, the event was structurally interpreted as though it contained a certain linear, chronological development with a beginning, middle, and end, resulting in a "homogeneity in topical emphasis" as well as a typically melodramatic genre structure (Brown 1990, 223). The main emphasis, however, in the U.S. reconstruction of events was on the motivation of the terrorists themselves. While the Italian reconstruction of events focused on the social negotiation of defining the event as terrorist or not, in the U.S. reconstructions, the event was clearly defined as terrorist. What was being socially mediated and negotiated was the "intent" of the actors (compare with Lauderdale 1980), i.e., was media coverage the primary motivating factor of the terrorist, and by giving it to them was the media acting as an enabler? The issue surrounding the taking of hostages and prisoners became incidental to the main event.

U.S. Reconstruction

The discourse of terrorism surrounding the TWA incident is more obvious in its use of the theater metaphor. Rather than representing the process of social negotiation and construction of the incident's meaning (in the Italian case, via competitive discourses), the theater metaphor represents an attempt and opportunity to explain why terrorism happens in general and who the terrorists are. The incident is already assumed to be "terroristic," as though terrorism constitutes a fixed, uniform, phenomenon. Theater, in the text by Rubin (1986) (see Chapter 3), for example, is used as a generalizable concept. He mentions that "terrorist incidents are so heavily scripted" that "both sides" are "able to predict, within reason what will happen." There are many assumptions about the theater reflected in this text. To begin with, "heavy scripting" is equated with predictability, and predictability is considered to be a desirable and inherent feature of theatrical plots, unlike the plot construction characteristic of a Pirandello play. If predictability does not occur, then "disasters happen." The overall assumption inherent in this text is that all terrorist plots (the TWA providing but one example) are basically the same and that theater is the best way to represent its plot.

Brown (1990, 225) notes with regard to the TWA incident that,"Shortly after the hijackers took control of flight 847 by gunpoint, they identified themselves as Shiites and demanded the immediate release of Shiite prisoners in Israel." Later on, Brown (1990, 227) suggests that "The terrorists who hijacked TWA Flight 847 initially appeared to be concerned about spreading their Islamic ideology, but the events that unfolded revealed the importance of their political intentions. The Shiite terrorists wanted not only the release of fellow Shiites held captive by Israel and two other nations, they also wanted to strengthen their political power base in Lebanon." A text by Smith (1985, 22) in *Time Magazine* suggested the same thing as Brown, only five years earlier. He wrote: "The terrorists' repeated emphasis on seeing officials of Amal, the mainstream Shiite organization, suggested not only that they were seeking a negotiated settlement but that their motivation may have been essentially political rather than ideological." A *Newsweek* writer concurred by stating that "No one knows how far the fired-up Shiites will go in their quest for . . . political power—or for revenge (Deming 1985, 25).

The attempt to define the act in terms of the motivation of the terrorists as an attempt to gain political power by "purg[ing] Western influence from the Islamic world" (Deming 1985, 10) is clear with regard to U.S. retaliation. As Former Under Secretary of State Lawrence Eagleburger stated, "Our failure to strike back will encourage more and more attacks on us." Furthermore, he noted that "revenge under certain circumstances is a perfectly legitimate act of state." Accordingly, President Reagan claimed that "America will never make concessions to terrorists." Yet Reagan proceeded to conduct behind-the-scenes negotiations with the Shiites. While this action on the part of the state appeared to be a complete departure from the typical U.S. foreign policy response of using force, it is important to note that it was around this time that the U.S. Enterprise (via Secord and

Hakim of Iran-Contragate) was selling arms to Iran (see Moyers 1990). When the controversial trade was exposed, the Reagan administration attempted to explain their actions as an attempt to protect and/or save the hostages in Lebanon (Tower, Muskie, and Scowcroft 1987). The state was defined as reacting to the incident.

There were also a number of confounding factors that defied a linear narration of the event, but appeared to have no effect on the reconstruction that ultimately predominated. The hostage crisis of 1979 in Iran ultimately sabotaged Carter's Presidency. He was criticized for not acting with force, thereby contributing to the United States' international vulnerability. The TWA crisis provided an opportunity for Reagan to demonstrate his strength as a leader, a superpower representative—at least in appearance.

The metaphor of dramatic theater as applied to the TWA incident projects a singular view of a highly complex and diverse form of aesthetic representation. It also informs us of a normative view that all human behavior should be predictable and must be controlled via systematic means. The assumption here is that all drama is predictable, therefore resolvable. The notion of predictability provides a code word for the prominence of a scientific understanding of reality, despite the use of the theater metaphor. Because predictability is desirable, a certain preference for texts written in scientific code is reified even if the texts are called "scripts" (which is a theatrical code). White (1987, 193) discusses the use of code shifts not as a matter of the author's particular writing style but rather as a process

by which a specific subjectivity is called up and established in the reader, who is supposed to entertain this representation of the world as a realistic one in virtue of its congeniality to the imaginary relationship the subject bears to his own social and cultural situation.

In effect, Rubin, Brown, Smith, and Deming, despite their dramatic representations, write within a scientific code, giving priority to it, and attempt to grasp and control the aestheticized dramatic codes within it, not allowing that the latter might have an excess that overflows their own or that their own departs upon the functioning of an aesthetic.

Media texts on the TWA incident in the United States used aestheticized speech often, although its use was more limited than the theater really allows. This was simply because the stories or event reconstructions were organized and presented in a narrative structure, even though the event itself defied such boundaries. While the theater opens possibilities of thought via aesthetics and artistic re-presentation to overtly question, blur, or challenge the moral and political boundaries of a society, terrorism re-presented as theater in the United States does not. As is demonstrated with Rubin's use of the theatrical metaphor to re-present the TWA incident, terrorism provides the type of drama in which moral and political boundaries are reified and reestablished (see Ben-Yehuda 1990; Goode and Ben-Yehuda 1994). Indeed, by shifting codes from theatrical to scientific, a certain distrust for figurative, blatantly aesthetic speech is introduced.

While the Italian press is perhaps less disguised, or more openly celebratory of metaphorical play in writing, the U.S. press works hard to affirm and bring to life the ideal of literal speech. The media in the United States claim to present or report objectively "the facts," as though the discourse used is uninterpreted, untransformed, and unaestheticized in its representation of reality (Wagner-Pacifici 1986, 283; Gusfield 1976). This conception or understanding of literal discourse versus figurative discourse reflects the dominant dichotomous view in the United States on art and science: they are viewed and treated as two completely different and separate enterprises. While the former is considered to practice techniques of embellishing, exaggerating, or distorting the truth in order to obtain an effect, the latter is touted as being in the practice of providing "truth." Thus, literary writing is concerned with "how" its subject is described in order to achieve a certain effect, giving autonomy and vitality to the aesthetics of writing. Scientific writing, on the other hand, is concerned with the subject itself, regarding language as merely a medium by which that subject is reported or described (Gusfield 1976). This dichotomous representation between the language of science codes and the language of literature or art codes has been noted by Hofstadter (1955, 294–5) as the following:

> The character of the imaginative object achieved by the artist depends on the character of the language he employs, whereas the language of the scientist does not operate within the involvement pattern he formulates.

Yet, as other writers and researchers have pointed out, the differences between science and art, literary and figurative discourse is more imagined than real. Each of these enterprises uses language and language can *never* be neutral:

> Anything that makes a functional use of words will always be involved in all the technical problems of words, including rhetorical problems. The only road from grammar to logic, then, runs through the intermediate territory of rhetoric. (Frye 1957, 331)

Gusfield's (1976, 17) work on the "Literary Rhetoric of Science" provides an example of the art involved in scientific presentations. He notes that "the [scientist] writer must persuade the audience that the results of the research are *not* literature, are *not* a product of the style of presentation. The style of non-style is itself the style of science." The distance between art and science, therefore is more a matter of style of presentation and representation than a matter of essences. Paradoxically, the texts on the TWA incident attempted to depict the actors as terrorists, and terrorists more generally as (actors) artists. In the following passage by Rubin (1986, 26), for example, the "terrorists'" desire to gain control of the situation is likened to the "Wizard of Oz":

> [M]enacing and frightening from out front, but behind the scenes really rather inconsequential figures pulling at a set of levers.

The analogy Rubin uses is valuable because he projects his own literal view of what the Wizard of Oz represents and then goes on to define him as "inconsequential." Rubin does not consider his own act of writing as a tool (such as the Wizard's tools) of power, or a way to "seek leverage," and "influence beyond (his) actual means or strength." Furthermore, by defining terrorists as inconsequential, Rubin accords more power to their acts than to them. It is as though his act of writing and interpreting is not what is aestheticized here; it is the terrorists action that is aestheticized. Brown (1990, 228) similarly discusses Berri's rhetoric as including persuasive elements, and it was these "persuasive" elements that garnered public support for his cause: ". . . Berri's rhetoric as the hijackers' representative can be assessed by evaluating Berri's merits as a storyteller, the appeal of his narrative and the media's ability to enhance his story." Again, the terrorist's action is the focus of aestheticization, and the media's role is secondary, as enhancer, not as co-creator (Ericson, Baranek, and Chan 1991).

Paradoxically, in attempting to discredit terrorist action by describing it as merely aestheticized action, these writers have accorded the terrorists' "intent" to do harm a greater sense of ambiguity, complexity, and, therefore, power. Rubin, for example, compares hijacking to political assassinations, claiming that the former "can get the juices flowing much more vigorously" than the latter, which may only happen "occasionally" (compare with Ben-Yehuda 1997). The killer of Israeli Prime Minister Itzhak Rabin and the actions of the Unabomber in 1995 are discredited for trying to attract the public's attention, which is what Rubin believes to be the terrorists' real intent, minimizing their action in exchange for their perceived intent. Rubin's selectivity in discrediting certain actions while amplifying others is not only a practice of his own power; additionally, he is providing an assessment for terrorists concerning what action is more effective. One of his suggestions, for example, includes a "busload of children." Rubin admittedly uses the theater metaphor as a strategy to demonstrate the "true" nature of terrorism so that it can be eliminated. It is obvious from Rubin's statement that one essential feature of the theater is forgotten—that it pro-

vides vast possibilities for interpretation—and that he only utilizes one possible interpretation, representing the theater and
the artist as monoliths. In the end, such a re-presentation is quite
problematic in attempting to eradicate terrorism. It may also
encourage it, even if unintentionally. In essence, writers have
various levels of political power and influence in their
artistry.As the scientist attempts to interpret or re-present
his/her findings in a particular form of discourse, privileging
certain rhetorical forms over others, so the artist (literary or otherwise) attempts to represent his/her vision of reality via the
appropriate medium.

The shifts in code characteristic of Rubin's text downplay
his use of literary metaphors and emphasize the scientific
dimension, which will enable his article to be trusted and taken
seriously. After all, he is attempting to provide an antidote for
the disease called terrorism. Interpreting the TWA event is incidental to his larger purpose for writing the text. It is clear from
his form of discourse that even though art is widely appreciated
in the United States, it does not have the prominence of science
in representing reality.

Science as interpreter of objective truth supersedes art as
interpreter of reality. When the news media report events that
require an additional commentary or analysis to further the
audience's understanding of the events, typically the explanation of a scientist is summoned. Despite the fact that numerous artists have represented terrorism in their works, how
many of them are asked to provide the analysis for a news
commentary? If terrorism is to be represented in theatrical
terms, would it not be more heuristic to have a playwright or
director provide an understanding of the terrorist theater?
Rubin (1986, 27) reflects the prominence of scientific control to
explain the "theater" of terrorism in the United States by
insisting that:

> [T]errorist organizations need a flair for the dramatic to
> sustain that interest. This requires changing acts, locations,
> demands and performers. . . . *To be effective, terrorists cannot
> strike too often in the same place or the same way . . .*

The above text says more about the marketing of terrorism than the theater of terrorism. The theater when it is successful presents timeless re-presentations that transcend location, demands, acts, and performers. The same is true for scientific representations. C. Wright Mills's (1959) work, for example is as relevant to many sociologists (and the study of social problems more generally) today as it was when it was first published. Similarly, a variety of films, plays, and novels are deemed "classics" to represent their timeless quality. What Rubin appears to be metaphorically representing is more of a contemporary economic view of society. This can be misleading if it is used as the most effective basis from which to understand, let alone predict, random acts of violence. Yet Rubin (1986, 24) goes on to argue that terrorists, like the government, want "predictability" (compare with U.S. Dept. of State 1988 and U.S. G.P.O. 1976). He ironically compares this "predictability" to theater companies who want to present something "stimulating," and not too eccentric or "repulsive" for fear of being "shut down":

> [P]olitical terrorists want to create a stir and attract attention without inviting massive retaliation by the government.

Rubin structures his argument on the theater of terrorism in a sequence characteristic of a typology or model for ordering reality. This method for ordering human behavior parallels scientific models and is viewed as a superior framework to art with which to understand human behavior. Rubin's writing slips in and out of the codes of these two frameworks so that his analysis of the TWA incident appears to be systematic and objective—represented as a scientific document.

Brown (1990, 222) also uses a typical scientific mode of explaining reality by suggesting that "Terrorists and their spokespersons produce two different kinds of rhetoric, that which appears to be cooperative and that which is antagonistic." He goes on to cite other researchers who make the same claims and have refined these categories as "persuasive rhetoric and coercive rhetoric." Then, Brown goes on to construct a typology using these two categories to explicate the rhetoric generated during the 1985 TWA incident. While the analysis is interesting and gives the illusion of providing some scientific understanding of terrorists and their motivations, so that responses to terrorism may be improved, it is an *a posteriori* analysis that makes generalizations about terrorism and terrorists as though they were a fixed entity and not a rhetorical construct (Ben-Yehuda 1990).

Furthermore, while the theater metaphor is used to try to understand terrorist acts, theater is not in fact appreciated as an alternative means by which writers such as Rubin or Brown might interpret reality. It is devalued and discredited in the same way that terrorist acts are discredited by virtue of the parallels that are suggested between the two phenomena. The action of terrorism is analogous to the "wizardry" of the theater in that in the end both are "predictable." By likening the theater of terrorism to "wizardry," Rubin distances himself from art and suggests that the essence of art is something intangible, unknown, mysterious, and therefore cannot be trusted any more than someone who can be defined as a terrorist who employs a similar tactic and therefore also cannot be analyzed. Rubin's own *art* is thereby immunized and cannot be exposed for its own arbitrariness, its own suggested violence.

Paradoxically, however, he attempts to reveal the wizardry of both the theater and terrorism by making it tangible, by attributing its magic to nothing more than the "art of amplification," and therefore not to be taken too seriously or viewed as unconquerable.

Texts such as Rubin's or Brown's accomplish two tasks. First, they reify a separation between art and science. By making terrorism analogous to art, they denounce both at once. The means by which to resolve terrorism as analogous to science, however, exalts the latter as though there is no art in science nor science in art. Second, this denouncement is accomplished by equating what is defined as an evil activity, terrorism, to the theater and attributing the rigor and accuracy of their interpretive analysis to science. In the end, science is depicted alongside the state as the necessary factor to the resolution of a plot.

As with the Italian theater of terrorism, a plurality of information is also considered to exist in the United States. Their differences, however, are content specific. Whereas in Italy, various types of plots are represented by using the theater metaphor in the attempt to find a representative structure, in the United States the theater metaphor is used to represent the same plot structure with different stories—hence the changes are superficial, involving the location or performers (as suggested by Rubin), but the action of the plot or story development is the same—terrorism. Most contemporary texts in the United States on "terrorism" (or "terrorist" events) define it as a multifaceted concept which can be examined according to the rules and assumptions of scientific analysis. Indeed, some texts on terrorism almost ritualize the regulative ideal of its objective understanding (Hobsbawm 1969; Bell 1974, 1978, and 1994; Russell and Miller 1977; Cooper 1978; Crenshaw 1979 and 1983; Gurr 1980; Wardlaw 1982; Wilkinson 1986 and 1990; Pisano 1987; Stohl 1983 and 1988; Schmid and Jongman 1988; Shultz and Schmauder 1994).

These texts also have provided theories for numerous manifestations of terrorism as well as empirical work in support of these theories (Arendt 1969; Walzer 1977; Shank 1987; Crenshaw 1995; Sharif 1996). According to these writers, terrorism is a phenomenon that utilizes violence as its means to either undermine or to maintain and strengthen the existing social structures and orders. As such, it can only be analyzed at one level of analysis. Thus, terrorism does not occur within domestic abuse relationships (even though victims are being terrorized) because it is a different, or wrong, level of analysis. What is left, then, is a reductionist explanation of "terrorism" which emphasizes motivations for such action, rather than explaining the latent structure of politicality, which enables constructions that create, maintain, or change the definition of terrorism (see Brown and Merrill 1993; Inverarity 1983).

This type of analysis, focusing on "why" a particular act occurs, continues to dominate in the study of deviance, more generally, even though research focusing on a political analysis of the definitions of deviance has more explanatory power. The problem with the latter type of research, however, is not analytical but practical. The process of social negotiation is not considered to offer any pragmatic resolutions to social problems and deviant behavior such as terrorism. But the emphasis on intentions and motivations assumes and justifies a "quick-fix" solution to the problem, characteristic of the short-term, short-sighted, political policy construction of the state.[1]

Within these two basic categories or motivations for terrorism (that is, terrorism as a phenomenon used to either undermine or strengthen social structures and institutions such as the state) are further subdivisions with more types, categories, or motivations for different types of action that can also be defined as terrorism. Concrete parameters and criteria are delineated so that we may readily and objectively identify terrorist action not only in general, but also specifically, i.e., the type of terrorist action (Targ 1988; compare with Gibbs 1989). From this type of research emerge the popular profiles of terrorists: victims of deprivation, religious or ethnic fanatics, ideological, issue-oriented, or state terrorists, to name a few types (Corrado 1988; Schmid and Jongman 1988; Sthol 1988; Schultz and Schmauder 1994; Smith and Morgan 1994).

Despite such detailed typologies, however, "terrorists" still manage to elude researchers attempting to further refine these categories and those who continue to define the use of social control as a response to the action. The approximately twenty-year existence of the Unabomber in the United States provides but one known example of this elusiveness and of the inefficient reaction of social control forces.

Most media and academic sources, however, attest to the existence of these various manifestations or definitions of "terrorism." Such texts also typically define terrorist activity as violent action against innocent bystanders by persons who are weak, sick, and disenfranchised and want to gain political advantage. Terrorist "action" according to this definition is interpreted within an interest-group, pluralist frame of reference, although the framework is assumed to be so self-evident as to require no express consideration (Sharif 1996; Bell 1994; Schmid and Jongman 1988; Pisano 1987; Wilkinson 1986; Gurr

1980; Laqueur 1977). Yet, such a framework also can be (and has been) used to explain violence against children and spouses, gang violence, or any type of violence in which domination and control are the practice of power.[2]

Within this frame of reference, we are told how to determine if terrorism has occurred. Duvall and Stohl (1983, 183), for example, suggest the following "rule of thumb": "we must be able to determine whether the intent of the action is simply to cause that physical harm or rather thereby to induce terror." Terrorism, according to this definition and interpretive framework, has occurred only when an actor intends to induce intense fear, to "alter a target's behavior or character." Yet, as some scholars have explicated, "intent" itself is socially negotiated (Lauderdale and Cruit 1993; Ben-Yehuda 1990). Considering intent as socially negotiated sheds new light on some of the examples most often cited to demonstrate terrorism *par excellence*. Terrorism, for example, is often associated with distant, foreign regimes depicted as completely different from the U.S. state. The Pol Pot regime in Kampuchea, and those of Amin in Uganda, Allende in Chile, Castro in Cuba, Khomeini in Iran, Quadhafi in Libya, Noriega in Panama, or Hussein in Iraq, to name a few, are cited as typically terrorist societies. They constitute "the other" type of political regime represented as radically different from the U.S. variety (Wilkinson 1990).

Newspapers and magazines in the United States with wide circulation, such as *The New York Times* or *Time Magazine*, unlike most Italian newspapers, do not openly claim any political partisanship. Rather, in the United States, the claim of "freedom of information" (or of the press) communicates certain background assumptions not only about the quantity and availability of information generated by the media, but also about the validity and acceptability of the information given (Miller 1982). The views and perspectives expressed by the media on any given subject or "plot" supposedly reflect the best possible interpretation of reality based on empirical "facts" and "experience," as though the latter are a natural political reality rather than a specialized code for representing reality. In this way, not only the assumption that a "neutral" language exists but also

the existence of a neutral politics is reified. The consequent public response and practical actions emerging as prescriptive
because of the way the plot is constructed are viewed as pragmatic, singular solutions excluding the possibility of alternative
insights or constructions.

In explaining and/or defining the plot of the TWA incident
as exemplified in Rubin's text, the term "terrorism" is used with
no ambivalence; on the contrary, terrorism is presented as a fact
unique to contemporary humankind, requiring unique practical
measures to suppress it, and the TWA hijacking *is an example* of
terrorism. The inherent assumption in the way Rubin presents
terrorism is the idea that it can only be understood if it is presented "objectively." Some writings are more obvious about
how they state this view. For example, consider Stohl's (1988)
book *The Politics of Terrorism*. It is acclaimed as uncovering the
"myths" that hinder "objective" study and as a resource
designed to settle the "controversies raging in this field" (compare with Zulaika and Douglas 1996). Between the two editions,
from 1983 to 1988, Stohl has even expanded his number of
myths associated with terrorism from eight to ten. Political terrorism is no longer an issue with which only the state must deal
in order to best preserve its legitimacy and authority over violence. It is now a field of study, a field within which various people become "professionals" or "specialists" at knowing and
identifying it (see Foucault 1979).[3]

Being able to identify the "terrorists" involves a complex
process of characterization. At a drama production, the development of the hero (or antihero) and the villain are indispensable to a successful plot. The following section examines the
development of the protagonists in the TWA incident and its
affect on the public's definition and identification of the terrorists.

One of the strategies which may be observed in the U.S.
texts on the TWA incident is the prevalence of a discourse
resembling the genre of melodrama, where good and evil are
dichotomized and depersonalized (compare with Brown 1990;
Wagner-Pacifici 1986). In reading such texts, the public can
respond simply by praising the hero and blaming the villain

without reflection on the psychological complexities of either. The public need not decide fault or grapple with what good might or could mean, as the decisions have already been made. All that is invited from the public is the ritual acceptance and denunciation of the hero and the villain reminiscent of a melodramatic production at the theater (compare with Wagner-Pacifici 1986).

Characterization

In a melodrama, the polarization of "good" and "evil" is exaggerated to the point where the audience is not asked or allowed to contemplate the morality or psychological natures of the characters or the complexities of the events or plot. The characters are in fact depersonalized and become objectifications of normative values. The audience is expected to praise the heroes and blame the villains. For the audience, the interchange between a very limited identification with the actors and/or a distancing from the actors of the plot is produced and encouraged.

Wagner-Pacifici (1986, 283) suggests that the use of melodrama is central to the "assertion of ultimate reconciliation" after the unfolding of the plot, in that melodramas clearly identify evil—in this case, a terrorist "other"—and remove it without contemplating whether the removal was even warranted. Such was the case during the Moro kidnapping in Italy in 1978, when the Italian state, the Church, the "intellectuals," and the media collaborated to construct the events in terms of the hero/villain dichotomy. This construction inevitably transformed the strength of a state, which since World War II had been in constant crisis, while weakening any form of dissent or opposition to it, whether by organized groups or individuals. Interestingly enough, by the end of the Moro event, the use of negotiations with the kidnappers was not encouraged by the state nor defended by the other collaborators, unlike the diplomatic stance of the Italian state during the *Achille Lauro* situation.

On the contrary, the American reports are definitive in identifying the evil actors, innocent victims, and heroic saviors.

Ironically, in this situation, the Italians were adamantly opposed to the use of force in dealing with the Palestinians (compare with the Red Brigades during the Moro affair, Wagner-Pacifici 1986; Drake 1995). The Americans, in dealing with the Shiites, were not only in favor of force, but consistently sought opportunities to provoke an armed confrontation, even though negotiations proceeded behind closed doors. Thus, such "negotiation" texts emphasize clear configurations of good and evil consistent with the melodramatic form. Furthermore, the prescriptive implications emerging from this genre appear to favor and justify the use of force in the elimination of the defined and identified "other":

> The Secretary of State's continued posturing (and the posturing of other members of the administration, including the President, because it played well in the public opinion polls, has been quite damaging: for example, in the aftermath of the June 1985 TWA hijacking, in which again the President did not unleash the U.S. force so often threatened, Mr. Reagan emerged from a screening of Sylvester Stallone's film *Rambo* and foolishly quipped that he now knew what he would do next time) has resulted in a situation in which the United States continues to appear indecisive and incapable of responding to the terrorist threat. (Stohl 1988, 585–6)

Stohl's characterization of President Reagan in this passage as the farcical leader entrusted to symbolize, maintain, and defend the American system is significant both for Stohl's immediate political practice as well as for the paradox it suggests about Reagan in recent cultural politics. Stohl is representing Reagan as "other" to the American structures and system by presenting him within the context of farce. He is suggesting that a character such as Reagan's is not to be taken seriously; Reagan is depicted as indecisive and silly. The structures of the American system, on the other hand, which he has been entrusted to protect and uphold, are not ridiculed by Stohl, as is Reagan, but rather are contrasted to Reagan. While Reagan is not being depicted as evil pitted against the backdrop of good (the structures of the American society), he is nevertheless being contrasted as dangerously silly.

The author's ridicule of the president occurs within parentheses, which further reduces and delegitimates his action, as well as the actions of the secretary of state. The president emerges as a rather pathetic individual who is to be blamed for his mismanagement. Stohl appears to be offering an *apologia* for having chosen someone so inadequate, an image creation of Hollywood as president, guardian and symbol of the American way, the American system. At the same time, the fact that the president did not carry out his "quip" is viewed as an embarrassment. He is characterized as someone who is not capable of reflecting the strength and integrity of the system and instead creates unnecessary problems (Iran-Contra). Furthermore, the president constructs his political policies around fictional movies such as *Rambo*. He himself is represented as fictitious or as an unreality created by Hollywood, which we are to disassociate or distinguish from the state and its structures, which are real and serious embodiments of our autonomy and sovereignty. By distancing Reagan from the state, we are asked to reestablish our credibility in the state because unlike Reagan it embodies a "natural" truth and therefore unquestionably represents a higher moral reality. The machine-like nature of the state itself, the unreality of the state's composition and operations is not questioned. The reader is merely expected to accept it as real and praise it (Baudrillard 1983a and 1983b).

Stohl's use of farce to depict the president allows the reader to first of all excuse his actions (or inactions), to reestablish the view that the problem in the American system is not the system itself but certain people chosen to run it (Moyers 1990), and to focus on the calculating retaliation of the "terrorists" in the face of such weaknesses in the American system. Also, in Stohl's attempt to delegitimize the president in exchange for promoting more consistent policies to deal with terrorism, he is also legitimating his own definitions and teachings on terrorism. His opinion, unlike the president's (equated with *Rambo*), is based on sound, empirical, systematic, objective evidence. Even though the contrast is weak, Stohl's point is obvious: scientific sources of information are superior to other sources (such as movies) which are not realistic (fantastical reproductions), therefore his truth is representative of the state's truth not Reagan's.

Paradoxically, while Stohl considers *Rambo* and scientific information to be opposite to each other—science as based on reality and *Rambo* as based on fiction or fantasy—he does not view the latter as a possible outcome of the former nor does he view simulations of war by the state or the military to be the same as *Rambo*. Ironically, Reagan is characterized as having the view Stohl repudiates. He estranges himself from alternative modes of interpretation and suggests Reagan as an archetypal example of one who derives his information from one of these alternative "other" sources. In contrast to Reagan, his own work contributes to truth and a serious body of knowledge.[4] It documents facts and figures, not aesthetics, and is written in the code or language of science (not the language of Hollywood), the dominant language of "reasoning, sovereign man," of truth.

Explanations of terrorism that rely on typologies are very common among many academic and other media forms of presentation (Brown 1990). A text by Cetron (1989, 23–24) exemplifies this approach (see also Schmid and Jongman 1988, for a comprehensive review of typological explanations, and Targ 1988):

> Fawaz Younis is a terrorist. He was the leader and spokesman for the group that hijacked and destroyed a Royal Jordanian airliner, and he took part in the hijack of TWA Flight 847 in which a U.S. Navy diver was killed. . . . Younis is typical of international terrorism today. He is motivated by deep-seated nationalism and religion; for that reason, his political movement has widespread popular support.

What Cetron is doing in his dramatic description of Younis as "terrorist" is constructing what has been termed a "psychological profile," which he claims is typical of international terrorists today. Many psychological profiles of terrorists have been constructed, all in the attempt to better identify the danger in our midst (compare with Crenlinsten and Schmid 1995; Smith and Morgan 1994; Wilkinson 1990; Corrado 1981; Burke, 1790, and compare to Russell and Miller 1977; Crenshaw 1979; Liebkind 1979; Hacker 1976; Crozier 1960). Cetron's psychological profile, however, does not characterize Younis as a person who may also possess characteristics of fear or love. He is a stock character who represents only one feature—that is, evil arising out of fanatical, narcissistic orientations and motivations (Lasch 1979). The implication is that if ethnic identity and cultural diversity are not controlled by some means, they threaten to destroy. The fact that Younis is chosen as the example instead of an American who may also possess fanatical feelings of nationalism and religion clearly identifies terrorism with Arab fanaticism, which according to Cetron is widespread. The history of the United States and its struggle for independence from Great Britain is replete with political actors who easily could have been given psychological profiles much as the one given to Younis, but the former are not defined as terrorists or psychologically deranged (see Lauderdale 1980).[5]

Former French Prime Minister Jacques Chirac was quoted by Cetron (1989, 24) in his attempt to further construct a psychological profile of terrorists. Chirac is instructive about negotiation tactics with terrorists and re-presents them as vacuous, selfish, instrumental entities:

> When you negotiate with people who take hostages, you are obliged, in the negotiation, to give something. . . . Once you have given something, the kidnapper gains from his action. So what is his normal . . . reaction? He does it again, thinking that it is a way of obtaining what he cannot obtain by other means. . . . That's why I don't negotiate.

By quoting the French prime minister, Cetron is suggesting that his assertions about terrorism possess a certain coherence both in time and space. Not only does the French leadership view terrorists in the same way as Cetron, but he quotes the *former* French prime minister, rather than the present one, establishing a historical and geographical continuity to his claims. Had Cetron quoted the present prime minister's policy regarding terrorism (which does not differ significantly from the former's), his claims would be viewed as perhaps valid across cultures, but not necessarily across decades. Thus, using force to manage the problem of terrorism is not just a typically American (U.S.) solution to international crises, but also a typical French response.

Chirac's claims about terrorism also confirm and expand on Cetron's portrayal of terrorists as objectifications of evil who do not merit analysis beyond their own greed-driven, criminal desires. Once again, as with a melodrama, the character of the terrorist is viewed only in terms of actions, not social or political essences (Barthes 1977). This representation may also be observed in a *Harper's* article, which states that "by replacing what he does with what he says," the media transforms "the terrorist's bloody theatrics" into political statements. (For examples of terrorists as "actors" see Goldaber 1979 and Crozier 1978.) In Chirac's depiction, the terrorist is reduced to the likes of a Pavlovian dog who responds to the appropriate stimulus— that is "gaining something." The implication of such a representation is that the reader will avoid identifying with the human person who comprises the terrorist. To look beyond the latter would be to invite ambiguity (both by the author and in the audience's response). This can be a particularly relevant paradox for a public whose historical and political pride is located squarely in the rhetoric of violent revolution, the power of independence, and even the religious myth of Americans as a "covenanted people" (successors to the apostate Jewish nation as God's chosen people; see McLoughlin 1978), so prominent a part of the United States' cultural core.[6] Thus, it is important for Cetron to establish what may ultimately be viewed as a criminal, apolitical orientation to his profile on terrorists (Merton 1968; Lauderdale 1980). The audience then can distance itself appropriately from the description and justify the removal of those who fit the description.[7]

Nabib Berri, the spokesperson for the Shiites involved in the TWA incident, gained much media attention. While his rhetoric used more symbolic terms such as "liberty," "justice," and "family" to gain U.S. public sympathy, the other Shiite men involved were projected as fanatical, nationalistic, and alienating, therefore deserving of retaliation (Brown 1990). In the end, the media portrayed Berri as a peacemaker and scapegoated the other two Shiites and the "terrorists" (see, for example, *Newsweek* 1985, 20 and 25).

The political objectives of terrorists are deemphasized in exchange for emphasizing their distorted minds, narcissism, desires, and actions. By attributing to them some political purpose via religious fanaticism or "deep-seated nationalism," however, the reader can view the terrorists as "rational" actors rather than simply as mad (Ben-Yehuda 1993; Corrado 1981; Walzer 1977). This strategy eliminates most opportunities for sympathy or empathy for the "terrorist." On the contrary, it represents him in terms of Machiavelli's cold-blooded tyrannical prince who was rational in his belief and proclamation that the ends justify the means (Bondanella and Musa 1979). The development (or lack of development) of the character of the terrorist allows the reader to view her/him very simply as a "criminal" devoid of any higher moral purposes (compare with Lauderdale and Oliverio 1995).

One of the criticisms of the media's reporting terrorist events is that they provide an avenue for legitimating the terrorist's action by allowing him/her to speak or to be heard (Brown 1990; Tower, Muskie, and Snowcroft 1987; Larson 1986; O'Neill 1986; Rubin 1986). The media have, in fact, been credited with transforming the terrorists' criminal behavior into one of a higher moral objective, a view that is expressed in the text from *Harper's* (1984, 43):

When Yasir Arafat spoke at the United Nations some years ago with a gun in his belt, he was giving a performance in what has become the terrorist theater. Every schoolchild knows the script: the terrorist . . . stands as a peculiarly modern hybrid of cold-blooded killer, glib ideologue, and fast-talking advertising man . . . the erstwhile thug emerges a "guerrilla" or, better still, a "freedom fighter."

In this text the media, particularly television, are held responsible for legitimating terrorist violence. The terrorist is viewed as making political statements, a political deviant (Merton 1968; Lauderdale 1980) rather than a "cold-blooded killer." Thus: "the media become indispensable partners in terrorist productions." This text is taken from a series of interviews with various prominent U.S. reporters, including Ted Koppel, Bob Woodward, and Charles Krauthammer, who discuss how the media can report terrorist acts without advertising terrorist causes. Furthermore, prefacing the interviews are two essays that examine/establish the *difference* between "terrorism" and "legitimate political violence," as though the two terms comprised a definitive, antithetical reality that could be abstracted and empirically tested (Lauderdale 1980; Ben-Yehuda 1990).

The structural presentation of the *Harper's* article is not without certain very definite political assumptions and implications. To begin with, the claim that the media provide an opportunity for terrorists to advertise their causes further confirms a misguided notion about the neutrality of the media.[8] The media are viewed as presenting the "facts" objectively. And one of the ways in which they attempt to sustain the notion of neutrality and objectivity is to present "the other" side of the story. This further sustains the inherent assumption that stories have two sides, one of which is viewed as the "other" side. In this case, the cause of the terrorist, defined as "the other," is discredited before it has a chance to be aired. Ironically, because the media refer to the cause at all, they are viewed as objective, regardless of the mediated interpretation.

Presenting the article in *Harper's* as an attempt to consider how the media can report terrorist acts without advertising their causes conveniently sustains not only the notion of the media's noble intentions to uphold objectivity but also the notion that the best way to represent the terrorist "other" is via the experts. There are numerous ways to be objective in the presentation of terrorism. It is also a means by which it (the *Harper's* article) can present itself as objective and factual: it provides interviews with eight prominent journalists and two essays, one by a leading government official and one by a professor, establishing the boundaries, explicitly with the content of the essays and implicitly with the content of the form of the essays (i.e., as presenting empirical evidence to sustain their claims, therefore, being of scientific value), within which it is deemed acceptable by the experts to discuss terrorism objectively. By leaving the analysis of terrorism up to the experts, the threat of genre slippage is controlled.

In viewing the media as a "road to legitimizing" terrorism, the article also conveniently nullifies any attempt by the media to understand terrorism beyond the boundaries established by the state (Ericson, Baranek, and Chan 1987, 1989, and 1991). Thus, if the media were to present someone like Abul Abbas as possessing a conscience and as struggling for the political cause of freedom, it would risk being lumped into the same category as the terrorist or at best as the terrorist's unwitting accomplice. ABC was criticized for broadcasting the TWA incident in order to improve their ratings (Brown 1990). Once again, this statement provides a justification, reification, and resuscitation of the banal myth of objectivity while simultaneously controlling for possible slippages of ambiguous representation. Also, in reifying media objectivity, even though the media's method of reporting "terrorism" is consistent with the form of government and academic interpretation on terrorism (as demonstrated in the *Harper's* article), the public (and the media itself) still view the various media as bearers of the facts, unaestheticized and untransformed.

Another structural component with more direct implications is the explicit presentation of Yasir Arafat as nothing more than an actor in a theater. The metaphor of the theater is used to represent the plot development of the terrorist events as though it were a tragidrama. It, in fact, reifies the melodramatic genre through the characterization of Yasir Arafat. The reader is told almost directly to consider Yasir Arafat within the boundaries of melodrama by making a specific reference to the theater and his actions, but not his character therein (the structural essence of theatrical tragedy). This same aesthetic prescription is implied by Rubin (1986, 26) in his use of the theater metaphor as a framework within which to "come to grips with and perhaps devise methods of dealing with political terrorism," and his consequent description of character/actor development.[9]

> A political terrorist's first job is to get and hold the attention of the audience—not only to make a big splash on Broadway but also to have an impact out in the streets. We typically think of terrorists as having short-term goals, such as obtaining the release of prisoners or some governmental admission of guilt, but their most important objective is to attract an audience and deliver a message. . . . An act of terrorism without underlying political justification is as devoid of sympathetic potential as a play without an organizing theme.[10]

Rubin attempts to identify the genre of the subject of his dramatic analysis as tragedy, as though it involves a single type of theatrical representation. Yet in his portrayal of terrorism and terrorists as a "drama," as in the *Harper's* article, the form more closely resembles melodrama.

Rubin's article, like Cetron's and *Harper's*, seeks to characterize terrorists in terms of good and evil. The characters are stock entities who are described as "insisting" upon being something different—the implication being that the reader knows they are nothing more than a group of "common" criminals. Rubin (1986, 22), for example, depicts the violent acts of the Baader-Meinhof gang of Germany as a narcissistic staging rather than as a protest against injustice against the oppressed, which is what they claimed. He erases any possibility that "higher" moral objectives might inspire such acts of violence. He instead portrays the political objectives of terrorists as excuses to gain justification or sympathy, and he argues that what terrorists "really" want is different from what they say they want: what they really want is an audience and attention (Rubin 1986, 27): "Too often it is assumed that terrorists and their parent organization mean what they say and nothing more than that. The challenge is to move beyond the performance." Once again, those who commit acts of violence defined as terrorism are denied a psychological essence (other than a vacuous need to commit violence) that would make them a part of the politically "normal" human race. Not only is the evil discussed as belonging to the realm of the nonhuman, but it is also violent and, in claiming to possess a political purpose for its acts, pathologically egocentric. In this way, a sense of paranoia among the public may be achieved. If the evil is depersonalized enough, the notion of repeated arbitrary attacks for no reason other than to receive media attention can be attained.

In the process of depersonalizing the terrorists' discourse, there is a simultaneous process of depoliticization unfolding and being sustained. Even though the government is portrayed as the hero, Rubin's discussion of what he thinks the government should do to neutralize terrorists also delegitimates the government's own discourse and actions. The readers (or citizens) are not being asked to assess the behavior or judgment of the government. In other words, even though the readers are drawn in to cheer for the hero, they are not asked to identify with it, any more than they are asked to identify with the villain. The readers are simply required to accept the reality of a government or state as an impersonalized bureaucratic machine. Lasch (1979, 147) discusses this process as the "art of crisis management, now widely acknowledged to be the essence of statecraft. . . . Propaganda seeks to create in the public a chronic sense of crisis, which in turn justifies the expansion of executive power and the secrecy surrounding it" (compare with Goode and Ben-Yehuda 1994; Wagner-Pacifici 1986; Baudrillard 1983b).

Another example of this depersonalization/depoliticization of the characters of the melodrama combined with the spectacle of the melodrama itself is suggested by ultimatly interpreting the outcome of the "terrorist" events as producing only winners and losers. For example, even though the U.S. government abstained from using force in the TWA hijacking, it is interpreted as an aberration (even a weakness, as per Stohl), because force was considered, indeed provoked by the government, and therefore should have been employed. Furthermore, the release of the "terrorists" is viewed as a loss by the government regardless of whether the passengers were freed unharmed as a result.

This loss was especially evident in the aftermath of the *Achille Lauro* incident, when the Italians clearly prevented the United States from flexing its military muscle and then from making judicial decisions about the terrorists.

> The Treaty (1983) conferred upon them (the Italians) a clear duty to hold Abbas until we had been given a fair opportunity to present the evidence we had against him. We went in the middle of the night, we accumulated as much evidence as we could in 24 hours. We got a complaint, we got a warrant. We sent the papers to Italy with a summary of our evidence. We told them that more was coming, more is accumulating every hour, but they did not wait. They rushed, made a decision, and let him go. (Dept. of State Bulletin 1985, 79–80)

Paradoxically, collecting evidence in twenty-four hours to imprison someone for life (possibly) is not considered to be a rush to judgment, especially since it occurred in a society whose justice system is built around the idea of "due process." Furthermore, Rubin fails to mention the actors of the "drama" who prevented the use of military means, or violence.

The outcome of the incident was attributed arbitrarily to one factor: the "absence of time pressure," rather than to appropriate political decision making and tactics—thus showing the readers who the "good guys" were without further exploring their intentions, motivations, and goals. Again, this allows readers to be drawn in to sing the praises of the hero, without questioning why or how—the creation of depoliticized political participation.

Overall, a specific generic predominance can be observed in the examples of Italian texts compared to the examples of U.S. texts.[11] A homogeneity of perspective between the state, media, and public opinion may be ascertained in both examples; however, how this homogeneity of perspective may or may not be presented varies. While in the Italian texts the contrast between entities is personified and reified, the American texts seek to depersonalize the entities or characters. Terrorism and terrorists become conceptual abstractions for which we can define and supply concrete empirical evidence in support of their existence. The most notable characteristic concerning the nature of the texts that proliferated at the time of the TWA incident is the variety of terrorists called upon to illustrate the point that terrorists and terrorism are generalizable. Even the days following the Oklahoma City bombing in 1995 in the United States spawned numerous texts about similar happenings all over the world, establishing a conceptual continuity for terrorism.

Likewise, good and evil are not political constructs but manifestations of a timeless, spaceless reality. The American texts, in resembling features of a melodrama, reify this idea of the existence of a good and an evil by establishing and constituting the boundaries of human behavior. The actions of human beings are decontextualized, depoliticized, and depersonalized so that we cannot question the boundaries so established, but rather accept and praise them. Furthermore, a sense of chronic crisis is reified since we have no way, either politically or ideologically, to account or feel for the evil. All we can "feel" is the satisfaction of seeing it removed. Consequently, we exalt in the expansion of executive, formal means of social control and surveillance—ironically, further exacerbating the ideal we purport to sustain—freedom. Ultimately, protection and autonomy is supposed to come from the promise of transcendence through our sense of "reason," which allows us to know evil from good and, therefore, effectively suppresses all ambiguity. Yet there are bounds to reason within which it is acceptable to know and reason, and from which we are shielded (see Gramsci 1971, on "hegemony").

6

Props, Sets, Stunts:
The Global Transmission of Reality

Design techniques and aesthetic interpretation are indispensable to a theater production, and in the twentieth century the stage more completely than ever before became a world that the viewer could vicariously inhabit, as stage settings acquired a new reality (See Bentley 1968). While the unfolding of plot and the development (or lack of development) of characters may be viewed as the two most significant aspects of the theater, scene design and aesthetic interpretation in the form of sets, music, lighting cannot be underestimated. Not only do such elements affect the way the scenes build or develop, but also the movement of the actors can be heightened or obscured. Also, scenic and aesthetic interpretations provide the opportunity to evoke the emotional values of a performance and the audience. Music, for example, is considered to release the mood of a scene, while fluctuating intensities of light can transfigure an object and clothe it with all its emotional implications (Simonson 1968; Artaud 1958). Adolphe Appia, a designer who wrote about theories of the theater in the 1930s, found that music "supplied a norm which an artist could approximate until his settings were equally expressive" and

> that light was invaluable in its "infinite capacity for varying nuances . . . for its power of suggestion." (Simonson 1968, 27–35)

The use of aesthetic strategies is not, however, exclusive to the theater. To be sure, techniques such as lighting, music, and scene design, which exist at the visual and acoustic level, are facilitated by electronic media, television, movies, and theater, and usually have not been incorporated by the print media. However, reliance on visual and aural techniques has also changed the nature of narration and the representation of human subjectivity not only in the electronic media but also in the print media (Eco 1979; Jameson 1983; Goldschlager 1985; Pfohl 1987; Ferrarotti 1995). The focus is upon achieving effects from images that are fast-paced, interrelated vignettes such as in the television series *NYPD Blue* or in movies such as *Natural Born Killers* or *Pulp Fiction*, or texts such as those by Le Carre, Ludlum, and Cussler.[1] These texts are not characterized by a narration that develops linearly, with a beginning, middle, and end (in that order),[2] presenting clearly identifiable ideological configurations. On the contrary, such texts incorporate the new narrative mode which has been regarded as confusing and blur-ring ideological identity and historical origin (Schulte-Sasse 1987; White 1987).

Texts on terrorism, whether on television or in print, increasingly embody strategies that rely heavily on the dramatic effect of such image construction. However, the reemergence and celebration of reactionary political values in the 1980s, especially in the United States, led to a further development and/or trans-formation of the subjectivity fostered by the new narrative mode in cultural reproductions of terrorism. Texts on terrorism, while attempting to evoke a dramatic effect through their image con-struction, are infused with a presentation of ideas, facts, and truth that is in essence tautological, much like the structure of a political speech (Goldschlager 1985). Furthermore, (and para-doxically) this presentation of ideas and facts exploits the notion and intention of rational discourse. The presentation of words, images, statistics, and financial reports by the media as though they were facts open to falsification discloses nothing more than vacuous symbols used in the fabrication of reality. Thus, while the media attempt to present information on terrorism as though it is open to reason and argument by calling upon the categories established by "reason," it also perpetuates a pretense. As Gold-schlager (1985, 167) aptly observes on ideological discourse: "the lack of a verification or discussion process integrated within the text allows it to dissociate itself from reality, without getting into any problem of understanding or acceptability."

In this textual milieu, the principle of identity is once again absolutely applied, since the nature of tautological structure cannot be reasonably argued or falsified. Because it attempts to argue a simple and verifiable truth by blinding itself to other forms of truth, it effectively disqualifies, from the beginning, all opposition and all other modes of understanding terrorism while restoring sentimental and emotional responses and affinities to ideological understandings. In this chapter, the texts of the *Achille Lauro* and TWA incidents will be examined in light of the aesthetic practices (or "special effects") of simulation, speed, and narrative mode, which produce a certain type of meaning and reality to the state, international relations, and the notion of terror in the creation of deviants and foes. Furthermore, these texts will be discussed in terms of their significance for the representation and perpetuation of a principle of the state as a sovereign and just reality. This notion is a significant factor influencing the social control of the deviant forces of disruption and ambiguity, viewed as inherent in the "terrorist" other (Ben-Yehuda 1993; Der Derian 1990; Pfohl 1987; Schulte-Sasse 1987; Virilio 1986; Baudrillard 1983a and 1983b; Foucault 1979; Benjamin 1969; McLuhan 1964).

Simulations and Redefining Terror:
The Speed of Narrative

The resurgence of reactionary values in the last decade has led to a revival of the role of the state as a cultural political agent in the attempt to salvage hegemonic values, ideological identity, and the monolithic presentation of history.[3] The *Institute for Cultural Conservatism*, for example, made "cultural conservatism" the driving force of the 1988 presidential campaign. The essence of this conservatism was projected as:

[T]he belief that there is a necessary, unbreakable and causal relationship between traditional Western, Judeo-Christian values, definitions of right and wrong, ways of thinking and ways of living . . . and the secular success of Western societies: their prosperity, their liberties and the opportunities they offer their citizens to lead fulfilling, rewarding lives. If the former are abandoned, the latter will be lost. (Schulte-Sasse 1987, 123–4; see Deloria 1992)

This resurgence not only has been widely praised but also has manifested itself within mass forms of cultural reproduction in attempts to fix meaning.

Among the processes by which meaning is fixed and apparent ambiguities are erased is the process of identity construction (Lauderdale and Oliverio 1995). Defining international terrorists, whether they are people or nations, is directly connected to this process of identity affirmation because it effectively alienates and externalizes groups and entities (Said 1988 and Hugo 1988) and justifies the means needed to eradicate them—more violence in the form of increased surveillance and wars. Thus, "what gives definition to a diplomatic system . . . is not the structure itself, but the conflicting relations which maintain, reproduce and sometimes transform it" (Der Derian 1987, 106). Particularly in contemporary global relations, where the perceived "other" national and international threats have been rapidly changing, the choice focus is on simulations and models, to expose "international terrorism" in an attempt to affirm identity, superiority, and "legitimate" means of violence. Der Derian (1990, 304) notes the following:

Historically, the great powers have reached relatively high levels of normalization by forging concerts of power, reciprocal codes of conduct, a body of international law. But this tenuous identity as a society was dependent upon a common diplomatic culture, as well as a collective estrangement from the "Anti-Christ Turk," the "colonial native," the "Soviet Threat," and the most recent pariah, the "international terrorist."

International terrorism, therefore, is directly connected to the various processes of identity creation, such as the construction of the nation or the citizen, and/or educational institutionalization (Lauderdale 1995; Thomas *et al.* 1987).

In the face of a declining sense of identity, an identity that is significant not only for domestic but also international domination, strategies of simulation and speed have been useful to mediacracies in facilitating the expansion of reactionary values and executive power (formal means of social control) and the authority structures suggested therein. The practice of simulation as an endless procession of mass-mediated images of "who we are, what we desire and where we are going" (Pfohl 1987) not only provides technical and tactical power needed by the state in representing terrorist situations, but it also provides us with powerful identity-creating images and re-presentations of the "picture-perfect" world. Furthermore, such images can be interpreted in terms of practical political measures and enforced accordingly by agencies of social control, who are viewed as protecting the desires of a (silent) majority. Terrorism, for example, is often associated with stigmatized groups. Internationally such groups typically include Islam—Iran, Iraq, Palestine, Shiite Moslems—or any group of people who are little known and are therefore vulnerable to political/ideological constructions that estrange their culture. The U.S. State Department names Syria, Iraq, Libya, Algeria, and North Korea as among the major supporters of terrorism in the world today. In the 1990s the places deemed most dangerous for "Americans" to visit because of terrorism are Chile, Peru, and Columbia (U.S. G.P.O. 1991, 102–6). Indeed, American Express publishes a newsletter for business persons travelling to foreign nations. In addition to millions of dollars, the policy includes a crisis response team in extreme emergencies. In general, U.S. citizens are warned that they are most vulnerable to terrorism when they are visiting "other" places that either house strategic U.S. military bases, do not appreciate U.S. influence, or are involved in their own ethnopolitical struggles for national sovereignty. Such areas include the Balkan region and parts of Latin America and Africa.[4]

Yet a striking observation by former Attorney General Ramsey Clark (1993, 71) points to an important and disturbing paradox concerning the application of the term terrorism to stigmatize certain people in contemporary society. He indicates that "the things that create the greatest terror in life by far are rarely called terrorism . . . and the things that we call terrorism, horrible in human terms as they are, are overwhelmingly the acts of powerless people." In the *Achille Lauro* seizure and the TWA hijacking, the estranged cultures were Palestine and Lebanon, respectively. The following text by the U.S. Department of State, Office of the Ambassador at Large for Counter-Terrorism, and constituting chapter nine of Stohl (1988, 322), demonstrates this process of effectively recasting the image of Palestinians and the culture from which they derive as substantially different from our own (or, for that matter, any other culture in the world), making it easier to define them as deviant, as terrorists, as enemies (see also Pisano 1987; Wilkinson 1990). Furthermore, it constitutes the nature of the Palestinian national objective as the work of a few ruthless individuals who arbitrarily betray their own people:

> International terrorism of Middle East origin increased substantially in 1985. Nearly six of every ten attacks either occurred in the region or were conducted by Middle Easterners elsewhere. Palestinian groups—whether considered politically moderate or radical—increased their level of international terrorism by nearly 200 percent, accounting for 256 incidents, or one-third of the total.

The specific citation of Palestine allows the reader to focus on this cultural group as particularly problematic among the already problematic area and culture(s) of the Middle East. A few pages away, in the same chapter, the reader is guided to a further understanding of why the Palestinians are such a "problem" not only domestically and in the Middle East but especially for the rest of the world—it is because they are a problem for themselves:

> International terrorism motivated by the Israeli-Palestinian dispute increased dramatically in 1985 and accounted for much of the increase in Middle Eastern terrorism overall.

Attacks on Jewish targets inside Israel and the occupied territories skyrocketed to 170 from a total of 50 in 1984. . . . Attacks carried out worldwide by Palestinians more than doubled, with the Abu Nidal group alone accounting for 10 percent of these incidents . . .

Wings of the PLO loyal to Arafat also participated in terrorism outside the Middle East. The hijacking in October of the cruise ship Achille Lauro by the PLF was the most *dramatic* example. . . . In 1985 radical Palestinians continued to assassinate more moderate Palestinians. In early December, for example, a prominent Palestinian lawyer who favored negotiations with Israel was stabbed to death outside his home in Rammallah on the West Bank. Radical Palestinians are believed responsible. (Stohl 1988, 346–7 (emphasis mine)

In an estranged move himself, the author provides an assessment of why Palestinians as a nation are such a problem. It is, he says, as though they embody a sheer desire to be violent, similar to a common, apolitical criminal who delights in the power of violence.[5]

Ironically, such textual images and representations of the Palestinian population resemble the "divide and conquer" strategy that was applied to most of the American Indian nations, as a byproduct of Euro-American "Manifest Destiny." Intergroup wars and destruction among the Indian nations themselves was encouraged and recast as the actions of a "savage" population who at any time could arbitrarily turn against itself (Lauderdale 1995; Thornton 1987; Allen 1986; Wallace 1970). Furthermore, the images constructed of the Palestinians are offered in quick, rhythmic succession, detailing statistics that no more than symbolize systematic scientific findings (as do most statistical findings by the media that appear to be emulating "science" but in fact (mis)represent science more as an icon of "truth") as they ironically appear to ignore the power of this type of data in fabricating the reality needed. These practices inevitably estrange the Palestinian culture and effectively set it in opposition to our own.

Also, notions of terrorism as employing arbitrary, indis-
criminant violence from which no one is immune, not even the
"problem" populations, are reinforced. Even the empirical evidence generated by more sympathetic organizations such as
Amnesty International involving the numerous victims or casu-
alties of "state-sanctioned" (or otherwise) terrorist action and
detailed descriptions of tortures have the same powerful effect
as the images, anecdotes, and statistical reports of government
reproductions (Crelinsten and Schmid 1995).

Locating the problem of the Palestinians as a "world-wide"
problem allows an international alliance of forces to unite
against them in solidarity. However, their specific location as a
specific threat to the United States is also significant textually, as
it allows for the further justification of any "special" actions
against them by one victimized, sovereign society. This process
was particularly pervasive in the texts that emerged from the
Achille Lauro and TWA incidents in the United States. The spotlight was squarely focused on the U.S. passengers as the "real"
target, the "real" victims. Moreover, the spotlight emphasized
the American victims so much that most interpretations of the
events never bothered to mention who the other passengers on
either of the carriers were. From most of the American texts the
reader is led to assume that most of the passengers must have
been American or that Americans were the most victimized. For
example, during the TWA incident, the most elaborate media
reports containing the protagonists of the event were the interviews with the victims and their families (Wagner-Pacifici 1986,
293). Wagner-Pacifici (1986) suggests that such tactics by the
media are essentially aestheticized political interpretations but
that the general public does not perceive them as such. On the
contrary, images and simulations of the "terrorist" events are
viewed as the "natural" political reality or state of affairs in contemporary society, certainly not as social constructions.

The Italian texts that emerged from the Achille Lauro affair
reveal similar tactics. In the Italian theater of terrorism, more
variety can be observed. The printed media that supported the
U.S. position, shared by the Republican party, reported (or did
not report) the passenger list in the same way as the U.S. media.

Particular emphasis was also given to the American passenger who died during the unfolding of the event (especially in *Avanti* and *Voce*, compared with *Corriere della Sera*). However, the media that supported the position of the dominant party, the Christian Democratic party, consistently reported the number of passengers who were Italian compared to the number of other nationalities. Out of the initial (approximately) 700 to board the ship, the overwhelming majority were Italians, according to *Corriere*, and out of the 400 seized passengers, 275 were Italian and the "others were a combination of several different nationalities" (*Corriere*, October 9, 1985, p. 1). In one issue of *Corriere* they even went as far as to list all the names of the Italian passengers on board the ship (October 8, 1985).

The reporting by *Corriere* consistently reified two major positions reiterated by the Italian government to justify their method of dealing with the event. The first position was that the Italian government preferred the use of diplomatic means to resolve the problem, and the second was to reemphasize that the fate of the "terrorists" was not for the United States to decide, but was once again a problem of the Italian state. By consistently emphasizing the (variously reported) number of Italian passengers on the ship compared to other nationalities, the U.S. state as a justifiable, major protagonist was clearly discredited. Furthermore, the article called attention to the Italian state for its exemplary behavior in that, despite the overwhelming majority of its own hostages, whom the government was vigorously trying to save, it was not in favor of forceful or violent offensive means of action, which would only exacerbate the issue and alienate another culture rightfully entitled to seek political independence, as all other nations have sought at one time or another. Needless to say, and ironically, the latter position of the *Corriere* and the Christian Democratic government proliferated and led to a strengthening of the Italian identity and state, not by establishing contrasts between the Italians and the Palestinians, but by establishing contrasts between the Italians and the Americans—the Americans as using the same "terrorist" tactics they claimed to abhor in the Palestinians, and the Italian state as the strong, silent, peaceful mediator. It is no wonder then that the

Italian state, despite initial threats of a dissolution of the coalition, became stronger than ever for standing up to its superpower ally.

However, while all this heightened emphasis is placed on the representation of terrorists and their fatal, generalized violence, the disparity between the destruction caused by "terrorism" and the destruction caused by legitimate military actions (for which simulations prepare) is not generally reported. For example, in the case of the *Achille Lauro*, the three "terrorists" were Palestinians, two of whom were legally juveniles. One passenger was reported killed. The United States was adamant about using force (or more violence, if necessary) to resolve this situation as a means to deter similar future attempts (Cetron 1989; Stohl 1988). Three years later, an Iranian civilian airliner carrying 290 people was shot down in the Persian Gulf by a U.S. military ship that had been training on simulated battle situations. The radar on the ship was reported as working perfectly, but the training sessions failed to alert the military that civilian airplanes flew regularly in the area (Der Derian 1990). The loss of 290 people was reported as an error, rather than (t)error, even though the victims were innocent civilians, the attack was random (on an estranged culture), and destruction was massive compared with the *Achille Lauro* incident.

The Implications of Text and Tech(nology)

The proliferation of simulations and the consequent expansion of executive power that results are part of an inherent and deeply ingrained logic of statism and nationalism, dominating thought and defining boundaries for thought and action in society (Clastres 1977; Said 1988). Ironically in fact, the very structures that have provided for the alienation of certain individuals and groups defined as terrorist are reproduced by them. This idea was reiterated (simulated) in a novel by Le Carre, *The Little Drummer Girl*, which focused on the Zionist-Palestinian conflict: "Are you nervous in the theater?" "Yes." "It is the same. Terror is theater. We inspire, we frighten, we awaken indignation, anger, love. We enlighten. The theater also. The guerrilla is the great actor of the world." This passage by Le Carre suggests a number of ideas about terrorism itself and about the aptness of the theater (dramatic) metaphor used to depict terrorists (as actors) and terrorism (the genre). Furthermore, it provides an example of intertextual simulation which emphasizes how terrorists reproduce and sustain the very structures (and metaphors) used to define them. Also, and at a different level of analysis, the interplay or feedback between alienation and identity within a milieu of deeply ingrained notions and norms provided by the nation-state may be observed (Said 1988). The need for increased protection by the state can be justified and implemented. Cetron (1989, 24), for example, is convinced of the future need for expansion of police powers with regard to terrorism, as though this expansion will eliminate "terrorism" (compare with della Porta 1995):

Swamped by this flood of stateside terrorism, local governments and police forces will press the federal government to enact laws that allow extraordinary measures to be taken in certain situations. The new legislation will define terrorism and clarify the duties of federal and state authorities . . .

The practice of speed allows for quick definition, detection, and elimination of the terrorist enemy by the state(s) while the media including computerized texts, compete in their re-presentation of events. These occur live and/or in sequential, anecdotal-type images so the public can be there to witness the forces of "good" prevailing over "evil." Virilio (1986), in his book *Politics and Speed*, discusses the violence of speed. Distance, he argues is no longer related to territory and geography, but to electronic systems such as the media. Speed is an essential criterion affecting the creation and dissemination of weapons, communications, and decision making among states: "Unity is in the terminals. It is in the instantaneous time of command posts, multi-national headquarters, control towers, etc. . . . There is a movement from geo- to chrono-politics: the distribution of territory becomes the distribution of time. The distribution of territory is outmoded, minimal" (as cited in Der Derian

1990, 307). An example from one of the texts cited in this study, which echoes this essential preoccupation with time in dealing specifically with international terrorism, is provided by Rubin (1986, 26). Time, he notes, is one of the features that can either make or break a "terrorist" attempt with respect to both the government strategies employed and the success of the terrorists' action:

> A passenger plane hijacking demands immediate attention, but the Achille Lauro episode gave the various governments ample time to develop a reasoned response to the terrorist demands and to resist succumbing prematurely to terrorist pressure.

Despite the fact that ample time was not the factor that kept the United States from using force, the passage affirms the possible justification for the use of force in situations where time is not considered to be a luxury. While in hindsight Rubin credits time for the resolution of events, had the event included force, would he have interpreted the events differently? What is misleading about his statement is that while he recognizes that time is an essential feature of politics today, it is not often the deciding factor for use of arms or diplomacy. Use of force and surveillance techniques is already set in motion; the question, as Virilio (1986) suggests, involves how efficiently force can be used, not whether or not it should be used. Cetron (1989, 23) also recognizes this need for speed in his observation of security techniques around the world: "Police, military, intelligence, and security people are on alert now around the world. They look for concealed weapons, check for correct ID and passports, and watch borders for movements of known terrorists or suspicious characters."

But beyond "speed," which is inevitably essential for strategic military purposes, and which has transformed the space and pace of international relations, for the purposes of the media speed is also a significant strategy. The frequently cut, interrelated, emotionally charged images presented by the media, which proceed in a logical sequence with an interpretation and reinterpretation of events, essentially possess a tautological structure. The interchangeable content of the images and their circular development increase the ideological impact of the interpretations. Furthermore, the drama of the image becomes much more important than analysis and information. Nowhere was this competition for dramatic effect in the interpretation of events more evident than during the Persian Gulf War. As news is a particularly hot commodity today, competition abounds over the way information is sorted, structured, and rapidly delivered from anywhere in the world (Ericson, Baranek, and Chan 1991). Said (1988, 56), in his observations of the effects of domestic electronic media coverage of the non-Western world in the United States on public attitudes toward foreign policy, notes that the

> almost perfect correspondence between the ideology ruling the presentation and selection of news . . . on the one hand and prevailing government policy on the other, maintains a consistent pattern in the U.S. imperial perspective towards the non-Western world. As a result, U.S. policy has been supported by a mainstream "identitarian" culture that has not been noticeably forceful in opposing its chief tenets . . . most of which is compressed into the word "terrorism." Out of this has come a stubbornly held conviction that American power in the world is the sentinel of freedom . . .

The presentation of events via satellite has much to do with the way the media are able to portray themselves as enabling the public to be at the scene or resolution of events, even though public access to the media is, in fact, limited (see Miller 1982 for an excellent review of news coverage standards for journalists). Virilio (1986) refers to this type of competition as a war of perception and representation, which he argues is increasingly replacing the reality of the battle site with a notion of the battle sight (Der Derian 1990). Schulte-Sasse (1987) further comments on speed, narrative structure, and its political/aesthetic effects as encouraging a politics of "disinformation" and a short memory:

Today's living space is obviously a fragmented one; the prevalent mode of spatial organization is duplication or repetition, which destroys the linearity or finality of space. The list of contributors to the synaesthetic fragmentation of human environment is a long one; uniform architecture . . . mass transportation and the experience of speed, which has the effect of fragmenting and aestheticizing landscapes, companies' habits of constantly transferring their employees . . . the effect of television on the production and organization of young people's spatial experiences.

The transmission of "live" on-site reporting is becoming of increasing significance in Italy as well; however, Italian media often rely on secondary information such as American "live" reporting from abroad rather than sending their own reporters (see Lumley and Schlesinger 1982), although this type of "second-hand" reporting by Italians is rapidly changing. Furthermore, the news and the comment about the news are not considered to be two different aspects, so even when live reports or journalistic interviews are provided, the interpretive, subjective nature of the reports is openly prefaced (Lenzi 1981) and publicly acknowledged. The obvious problem with interpretations of interpretations, or interpretations of events that are far enough removed in time that the events themselves are not remembered, is that, once again, the public derives its information and perspective about "international terrorism" from sources that have little or no resemblance to the original event. Specifically with reference to the *Achille Lauro* event, the media, both from Italy and the United States, were limited. Access to the ship was difficult and most of the information generated involved either speculation or interpretations of government-approved information (De Rosa 1987).

Even though strategies of simulation and speed could be effectively used to perpetuate a perspective of a "'neither war nor peace' situation that may be fraught with dangers but is certainly preferred to a shooting war," for the most part their development has been to prepare for war and other so-called "legitimate" means of violence needed to protect and sustain

American hegemony (Der Derian 1990; cf. von Werlhof 1989). The implication of the use of these strategies in transmitting information to the public and the rest of the world regarding events such as the *Achille Lauro* incident or TWA hijacking, therefore, is that they are more than just means by which we can know what is happening abroad. They are means by which the transmission of a discourse of terrorism will eventually lead us to know terrorism as constructed by the state(s) and supported by the media. Just as the theater utilizes props and stunts that oftentimes impress us and either draw us further into the plot or away from it, so the strategies of simulation and speed in textual constructions of "terror" and "terrorism" can envelop and mold our senses and perceptions of the world.

PART III

CONCLUSION:
THEMES, MESSAGES, REFLECTIONS

7

TERRORISM:
THE ART OF STATECRAFT

In 1980, an Italian lawyer who supported political activists in Italy remarked that "The victors have decided to tell the story of a generation through judicial procedure. It is an absurd pretension but they have done it and in this way the political conditions and the technical procedure have been created which mean whatever you say it is certainly criminal" (Wagner-Pacifici 1986, 286). Robert Kupperman, Senior Adviser of the Georgetown University Center for Strategic and International Studies, stated, "We can put more emphasis on preventive measures. For example, U.S. airlines ought not land in Greece. Americans have to be alerted that there are dangerous places in the world. . . . If we lash out blindly, the terror overseas will almost surely migrate to the U.S." (*U.S. News and World Report* 1985, 22). These remarks can be considered as a useful departure point for the analysis of discursive representations of ostensible terrorist incidents such as those involving the *Achille Lauro* and TWA. Terrorist violence must be understood not as a behavior that occurs as a result of cultural or psychological differences, nor only as a simple culturally constructed object of the human desire to maintain status as a subject, but rather as a semiotic difference.

Examining terrorism as a discursive practice in the art of statecraft reveals the inextricable link between terrorism and the production of power relations via the detailed descriptions, categorizations, and hierarchical organizations of contemporary society. It is a practice that privileges rhetorical language over direct experience. The value of analyzing terrorism as historically and contextually produced political discourse, rather than as essential human expression, is that it has the potential to be replaced by a more heuristic construct.

As a discursive practice of statecraft, it is understandable that the bombing in Oklahoma in 1995 is unquestionably defined and understood as an act of terrorism. It is also understandable, although seemingly counterintuitive, that the fact that approximately 10,000 people in the United States are killed annually by handguns remains ambiguous. As former Attorney General Ramsey Clark (1993, 71) explains, "The things that create the greatest terror in life by far are rarely called 'terrorism' . . . and the things that we call terrorism, horrible in human terms as they are, are overwhelmingly the acts of powerless people." The paradox is striking since the most semantically powerful construct in mobilizing human emotion and government action is reserved to condemn those people who are already marginalized. Research indifferent to or ignoring this symbiotic relation between the construct of terrorism and the discursive art of statecraft is at best naive and at worst grossly misleading.

The intellectual descendancy of the construct of terrorism is central: terrorism is understood not only as a discursive practice but also as a construction emerging from eighteenth- and nineteenth-century orthodox assumptions of man, nation-state, and political sovereignty. Terrorism analyzed as a historically produced phenomenon, the product of a particular political discourse rather than the expression of certain underlying and fixed human capacities and/or actions, has the potential to be transformed or disappear, as is the case currently in Italy (compare with Nash 1994). This latter point stresses the value of analyzing terrorism as a discursive practice in the shaping of both social theory and social practice. Namaste (1993, 193) explains this process in the following way:

> The circulation of semantic options within specific discourses and discursive formations has significant implications for the development of institutional policies and practices—operations which, through their deployment of select semantic options serve to frame conceptual and political issues. . . . Language as social semiotic, then, con-

stitutes "reality" not only in this purely linguistic sense (the act of naming), but also in a specifically social sense (the operations which do—or do not—develop out of that naming).

The theater provides a useful metaphor we can use in the analysis of the discourse of terrorism, not only because of the political/aesthetic reality it suggests, but also because of the boundaries it imposes structurally. The metaphor of theater with respect to terrorism, "revolution," and war is used consistently as part of the rhetoric of violence. But how it is applied in the rhetoric of violence can also have significant implications regarding public perceptions of and responses to events such as the Achille Lauro or TWA incidents and the appropriate means to define and resolve such situations.

Although the United States and Italy share common economic, social, and political interests, these sites of discourse emerge in two societies that are defined as (and consider themselves to be) different places, countries with different cultural backgrounds and different languages to represent the differences. But these differences are often not noticeable in the content of the texts—their contents, more often than not, express similar needs with respect to their national and international interests and sovereignty. What does differ, however, is what White (1987) refers to as "the content of the form," that is, the way the form of the text functions strategically. In other words, how certain practices of the discourse of terrorism such as metaphor, binary oppositions, genre, media selections and tactics, and modes of presentation work to fix ways of knowing and acting considered not only to be necessary to autonomous being but also of a higher natural political/moral order (e.g., the American Constitution); how these various strategies are involved in the social control of meaning, or practice of power from the standpoint of a sovereign subject (reasoning "man") who is considered to be the originator and creator of all history, all culture, and all truth.

While there is always the danger of overstating certain observed differences, this analysis suggests that in Italy the theater of terrorism may be understood to represent the competition among heterogeneous understandings of events, in the process or attempt to fix the meaning of those events, the process of social negotiation (see Wagner-Pacifici 1986). Publicly, "terrorism" is recognized as a political construct and part of the discourse of "judicial procedure" (compare with Lumley and Schlesinger 1982), which in turn is viewed as an arbitrary, political construction. Judgments and assessments made by and represented in the language of judicial procedure are not publicly viewed as emanating from a higher "natural" sense of truth, morality, and knowledge. Thus, the competition of meaning(s) that unfolds among the political parties, the media, and the government is recognized as a deliberate attempt to fix meaning in order to successfully manage domestic and international order. It is not necessarily viewed as a final resolution to the problem or a reconciliation that promises to settle all ambiguities regarding the nature of terrorists and terrorism. The fixing of meaning to an event such as the *Achille Lauro* affair is viewed and understood publicly as a political action, an act in the play of power. Politics may be understood, as Foucault suggests, as "an endlessly repeated play of dominations," as an endless power clash of multiple wills, interpretive dispositions, and projects within an *intrinsically* pluralistic world.

The construct of terrorism can be understood as a discursive practice in the art of statecraft by examining its desuetude in Italy. Since the Moro affair, violence in the form of bombings, killings, and hostage takings have occurred in Italy but terrorism as the category of defining the action has increasingly declined. Indeed, while the Italian Criminal Code defines various repressive measures, punishments, and penalties for terrorist crimes, it provides no definition for terrorism (Pisano 1987). Yet the Italian judiciary's direct participation in providing information on terrorists and terrorist action has been considered noteworthy in isolating, countering, and eventually defeating "terrorism." By the time the *Achille Lauro* affair occurred in the mid-1980s, even though a national symbol and entity of the Italian state had been attacked, terrorism was no longer perceived by either the state, media, or citizens as a destabilizing force.

The rhetoric and political response to terrorism in general, and specifically as manifested in this incident, had changed.

Today, in Italy, *la crise*, including high unemployment, inflation, overpopulation, government instability, depletion of natural resources, and violence, continues to plague the country. In the last few years, rather than defining terrorism (e.g., in the form of the Red Brigades) as the number one enemy of the state and its democratic institutions, corruption of the government in the form of *tangenti* (kickbacks) and, of course, the mafia are defined as the "real" threats.[1]

The struggle of the Italian state against the mafia is not new, and periodically reemerges. The Fascist regime of the 1920s and 1930s made the eradication of the mafia one of its central political policies. And about every ten years since the end of World War II, the state has constructed new legislative policies to counter the mafia (Pisano 1987). Chubb (1989, 1) notes the ostensible distinction between terrorism and the mafia:

> The difficulty of the Italian state in combatting the mafia arises fundamentally from the fact that the mafia is not, like terrorism, an external enemy but rather one which has succeeded in penetrating deeply into the very institutions which are supposed to be fighting it. It is this presence of the mafia within the very structure of the Italian state which renders it a much more insidious and ultimately a much more dangerous threat to democratic institutions than was the more openly subversive but more vulnerable and exposed phenomenon of left-wing terrorism.

Ironically, twenty years ago analyses of a seemingly impervious "terrorist" organization such as the Red Brigades, including its clandestine nature, its cell structure, its relationship to political power, institutions, and support as well as its deeply embedded roots in the history of Italian political culture, were very similar to the present analyses of the mafia, only today the mafia is considered to be even more insidious and impenetrable than terrorism (cf. della Porta 1995). Since the late 1970s, the Italian discursive struggle over the term, terrorism, and its apparent transformation (or disappearance) may be more usefully viewed as the product of a particular historical moment and political discourse rather than the manifestation of a certain special type of destabilizing violence.

In Italy, unlike the United States, it would appear that power and politics by and large do not appear as something negative, as a matter of limitation, constraint—something to be referred to when reason fails. The practices of power and politics are not other to truth. On the contrary, power is viewed positively, as a productive practice. It produces modes of subjectivity and corresponding modes of objectivity, knowledge. Politics is not something that issues from a source; it moves and evolves through practices and ways of understanding and being with the world. In this light, the state is not estranged and looked upon as the source of all authority, and therefore as something obvious; on the contrary, Italians consider themselves to be actively contributing to the practices of the state as well as their definition.[2] The theater(s) of terrorism in Italy, as we explored with the *Achille Lauro* affair, has exactly this effect: of sustaining the clash of multiple wills and multiple interpretations, as well as providing ambiguous, ambivalent meanings to the term itself. And rather than denying their strategic aspect, their political aspect, the theater, in fact, celebrates these aspects as essential to any social construction of meaning, which in the end is an act of politics.[3]

Because of the public recognition of this process, in Italy, while one construction of terrorism may predominate, "order" is not necessarily restored. Even though the state may appear as strengthened because of the way it handles a crisis such as the *Achille Lauro* affair, the state, above all, is not looked upon as an answer, it is looked upon as a question (see Foucault 1979). The restoration of order is often distrusted; it is often viewed as the desire of a state that is other to its contributors (its people), who in turn perceive such a move as inherently "authoritarian," inherently "fascist" (Grundle and Parker 1996). What may be considered (and defined) abroad, by the United States in particular, as political fragmentation, strife, and ultimately a "state" that is out of control, unable to harness the passions of its people, in Italy is understood as "active" political participation, as necessary to the *democratic* process.

In the *Achille Lauro* event, while a homogeneity of perspectives prevailed among the media and the government as a result of the "international" implications, a crisis of government did initially threaten to change the nature of the government as a result of their decisions. However, a change of government did not occur immediately following the event, as the celebration of Italy's unmoving political position (to not use force) in the face of a bullying superpower won out (De Rosa 1987). In fact, the success of the political practices themselves were celebrated even more than the resolution of the event itself (Munzi and Stagno 1985).

The American texts that emerged from the TWA incident also displayed a preoccupation with analyzing and defining the events in terms of a theater metaphor; however, American constructions of theater focused on the unfolding of the event itself. Theater may be understood as a metaphor representing constructions of "good" and "evil," suggestive of a melodramatic genre, rather than representing the *process* of those constructions. Events interpreted in terms of definite, timeless binary constructions and tautological structures furthermore engage the audience to either praise the so-called good or blame the ostensible bad, as though such constructions were based on a natural reality embodied by the forces of good (which is furthermore embodied in the structures of society). The implication of the theater metaphor as depicted in the American texts sets up a different sort of stage—one in which ritual and symbolic reaffirmations of identity based on difference and spectacle predominate.[4]

One of the ways in which this genre is made to prevail is through the use of science and the language of science. The implicit promise of the various disciplines of modern science is that they contribute to a body of knowledge that seeks to achieve the clarification of all ambiguity that has threatened to elude understanding and control. Knowledge in this sense is power, as its claims are represented as the ultimate truth, and truth is viewed as other to politics and power. One of the ways in which this scientific control has been established is through the ritual creation of dualisms and their presentation as though they are unaesthetic, untransformed, natural realities. The American media, as can be seen in the texts of the TWA events, are very skilled at presenting facts, statistics, and other scientific-sounding evidence and claiming that the language they use to present this evidence is neutral in the same way that scientific language is viewed as neutral. But "the facts" do not guarantee that the *form* of their presentation is any more innocent or apolitical than the language used to represent them, just as the histories we read, which are written largely by or for the winners but presented as a truth that is other than, or above and beyond, those who present it (White 1987).

Similarly, the state is understood to represent this position in its legitimate claim to expand social control and use violence. The state stands as separate from its people and defines what is criminal and what is political (as though the two can be separated) and acts on that surface according to how it defines it. The state is the means of coercive discipline and correction—it simply cannot leave people to correct other people themselves. As a consequence, power and politics are regarded as dangerous and as passing historical problems, much as "terrorism" is considered to be a unique problem of contemporary societies.

Practices of simulation and speed in (post)modern society provide for the preparation of what comes upon achieving total knowledge—how to quiet the forces that threaten and endanger that autonomy so achieved. For this purpose, technology provides us with models purporting to represent reality and the collapse of space, which means that geography no longer becomes an impediment to either our understanding of the world or our efficient removal of evil forces around the world. Even though these practices could be used to promote alternative perspectives on the violence that emerges as a result of war or other violence, their essence is not to promote peaceful relations among the dualisms so constructed. Rather, their essence is to promote the peaceful relations that are promised as a result of eliminating the "other" of the dualism.

The analysis of terrorism here does not eschew the boundaries that exist in the attempts to establish identity and knowledge in exchange for new boundaries, or pretend to offer a new approach that will allow us to eliminate or synthesize the boundaries. There is, however, a recognition that even the best efforts to explore (his)torical or even current events can be doomed by their own self-enclosure. The possibility of widening the space in which we see ourselves in relation to others becomes significant: "[I]t is to see and study (the boundaries) . . . as mythic markers for differences that we need but need not war over" (Der Derian 1990, 309).

In this light, we can examine the construction of events as multiple competing strategies, practices, and forms all striving to control meaning. Some strategies, which are considered to be privileged and representative of truth, are in fact obsolete, and other strategies that may have mattered in the construction of knowledge can be viewed as having defied understanding and detectability.

We can also consider our relationship to competing interpretations involving contemporary social institutions such as education, the family, the church and the political project they perpetuate, as well as the resistances and boundaries they need to surmount, if indeed they can be surmounted. Armstrong (1985, 8) suggests we consider, for example, "the various ways in which people read before we teach them to do otherwise." In exploring the discourses of terrorism from two different societies, we can in fact take Armstrong's suggestion seriously, to explicate how different forms of the rhetoric of terror affect perceptions of terror and the politically prescriptive implications of those perceptions. While an analysis of this sort tends to pose more questions than it answers, and the answers it offers are often considered to be putative or banal at best (i.e., that no stories about the past or the present are ever ideologically or politically innocent), it does offer new possibilities and paths for examining the histories of the "losers," which for whatever reason have been erased, suppressed, or controlled, as well as the more elusive strategies by which such control takes place (Colella 1989).

If we consider, for example, the heterogeneous example of the Italians in defining the *Achille Lauro* incident, and if we view the construction of meaning as an essentially productive political practice, exposing the acts and practices of the state rather than hiding or suppressing them, how might the American perspective about "deviant" or other cultures be "opened" to alternative understandings and constructions? Also, we need to consider underlying transformations in a society that may lead to discursive struggles over various political issues. Rather than simply examining the issue itself as though it were a representative social problem, the sources that lead to its construction and changing definition require examination. This is the case with terrorism in the United States today. Is terrorism the destabilizing force that threatens U.S. society, compelling us to seek out the terrorists as witches and eradicate them? Or are important transformations occurring as we approach the twenty-first century, which defy hegemonic or what are often considered to be "traditional" methods of analysis and understanding? Moreover, if we maintain the notion that there is no world beyond the political, beyond the plays of power (i.e., that the world is inherently composed of power relations) how might the celebration of alternative approaches to terrorism, as exemplified in the Italian case of the *Achille Lauro*, be amenable to the construction of alternative foreign policies that perhaps discourage offensive and forceful practices?

Certainly in considering some of the observations being made in this study, which in the end is also a practice of interpretation (as are all studies), the limitations of the interpretation must also be considered. How might alternative theoretical plans to the "theater" plan provide new modes of subjectivity beyond the bounds imposed by the theater metaphor? Or, if the analysis had focused on the practices of one society with respect to the rhetoric of terrorism, how might our understanding of power and politics as a productive, visible practice of the state have been improved?

While this study certainly provokes more questions than it answers, it also invites us to think about some of the practical problems raised when politics is made to be a visible action, one that can be celebrated and contributed to rather than regarded as negative, as a means of coercive discipline. Moreover, it attempts to relate this practical (theoretical) concern to the ongoing practices of societies—in this case the practices by which events become defined as "terrorist" and the definition viewed either as a part of political and social practice or as other to it—a judgment that holds the promise of controlling all ambiguity (as though the essence of ambiguity is evil). The practice of regarding the state as a question rather than an answer is not beyond the capability of some societies, as we have observed in the Italian case. And in comparing it to the practices of the United States and the perceptions of politics in the United States, we might begin to re-think and re-react to constructs such as terrorism when we acknowledge our own participation, our own practice of power, in its definition.

Since the end of World War II, the United States has directed much propaganda against its enemies (domestic and international, real and imagined); but in the end such propaganda has done little to encourage any kind of permanent solution to the problem of "terrorism," which it apparently seeks to eradicate. Furthermore, it has done so at the expense of the democratic process, which is supposed to foster competition among diverse understandings, ideas, and approaches to those ideas. Instead, the trend has been to encourage passive forms of collaboration from the mass constituency, increase autonomy of the executive from the legislature, as well as foster corresponding forms of representation based on such passivity (such as the "hero-villain" dichotomy) (Lumley and Schlesinger 1982). As Lumley and Schlesinger (1982, 622) remark on the elimination of terrorism, it is "something far more likely to occur through argument, discussion and open debate than through the counter-terror of the state," and other societal (political) institutions that encourage "exorcistic rhetoric and demonology." If "terrorism" indeed needs to be eradicated from society, then the eradication of orthodox perspectives and the forms those perspectives take appears to provide the most promising (if not crucial) avenue.

8

Epilogue

"All the world's a stage and all the men and women merely players."

—Shakespeare, *As You Like It*

In a government of laws the existence of the government will be imperiled if it fails to observe the law scrupulously. Our government is the potent, the omnipotent teacher. For good or ill it teaches the whole people by its example. If government becomes a lawbreaker it breeds contempt for law: it invites every man to become a law unto himself.

The above statement was made before the U.S. entry into World War II by a supreme agent of the state, Supreme Court Justice Louis D. Brandeis, who recognized the potential terror of institutional violence, before the United States decided to legitimate terrorism as a formal rational practice in the form of saturation bombing directed against civilians in European and Asian cities. Fifty years later, President Reagan issued the following warning to the world: "Let terrorists be aware that when the rules of international behavior are violated, our policy will be one of swift and effective retribution." And in 1995, President Clinton adopted a very similar stance by saying: "We have got to take steps aggressively to shut it (this kind of violence) down. . . . I'm going to do everything in my power to do just that." As a site of institutional violence, if the state continues to take its own terrorism for granted, failing to recognize the paradox, then, as Commanger (1985, 22) notes: "they should not be surprised when desperate fanatics, unable to wage traditional or 'legitimate' warfare emulate their betters."

Different aspects of the contemporary state have been examined and developed since Max Weber's (1958, 77) definition of the state as "a human community that (successfully) claims the monopoly of the legitimate use of physical force within a given territory." Gramsci, for example, develops the idea of hegemony as it relates to the state.[1] Foucault examines the state's relationship to power and knowledge. Geertz analyzes the state as a symbol of high authority, its display of status, pomp, and circumstance. Tilly analyzes the exploitative nature of statemaking and statemakers. In examining terrorism in the art of statecraft, each of the above aspects or meanings given to the state is explored in the discourse of terrorism and its prescriptive implications.

Few actions mobilize the emotive responses of fear and indignation more surely than acts defined as terrorist or terrorism. The media daily bombard our senses and sensibilities with information on various forms of violent crime that threaten the moral and social fabric of society; yet violence identified as terrorism is still viewed to be particularly unnerving. Consider, for example, a reference to domestic violence as "terrorism in the home," by the Health and Human Services Secretary of the United States (U.S. G.P.O. 1990, 118). Most social science research, however, views terrorism not as a practice of social control or domination but as a specific political phenomenon, a special type of violence: one that contains its own special structure and criteria. Practices such as kidnapping, bombing, assassination, hijacking, or sedition may be considered within the discursive purview of terrorist tactics, but practices such as rape, spousal or child abuse, racism, gang violence, environmental destruction, poverty, or even gross medical malpractice, to name a few, are not recognized as terrorism (Reich 1991).[2] It is no wonder, then, that the recent reference to domestic violence as "terrorism in the home" is viewed as little more than a sensationalized conceptual misuse of the term terrorism (a rhetorical, polemical tactic) rather than as providing substantive, analytical meaning at a different degree of abstraction[3] (Felshin 1993; U.S. G.P.O. 1990, 118).

Even genocide, as it has been practiced by many states, historically and comparatively, is often referred to as a "reign of terror," or "state terror," conceptually distinct from "terrorism" or defined as a subtype of terrorism (Ben-Yehuda 1993; cf. Gibbs 1989; Schmid and Jongman 1988; Huggins 1987; Petras 1987). Such a definition of "state terror" obfuscates the practices of the state, emphasizing only the state's more obvious repressive actions such as in prisons and illegal "law" enforcement. Other actions in hierarchical organizations re-presenting the state's repressive practices such as armies, hospitals, schools, or the media are not included in standard definitions of state terror.

An ancient Roman saying claims that *si vis pacem, para bellum* ("if you want peace, prepare for war"). Generations of people, in particular state leaders, have believed in and implemented this maxim despite the example of the wars that led to the annihilation and extinction of the Roman empire. And throughout history, the maxim has been shown to be false, time and again: the amassing of weaponry and military power has not brought about world peace but world destruction to the real economy, that is, the environment and life (Renner 1993; Lauderdale 1993).

From the Chernobyl incident, the world learned again the hard lesson that contaminated air, water, and soil pays no attention to the political boundaries constructed and privileged by humans. This incident terrorized millions; yet it was neither defined nor perceived as terrorist violence. Ironically, however, it also became increasingly clear that the survival and demise of our world often rests with negotiators, the artists of statecraft. For this reason, it would appear to be vital to understand this process of negotiation, of statecraft as it emerges and develops at different levels of analysis. Because every act of violence has the potential to escalate into a larger outbreak of violence, the art of statecraft must be more closely examined as a continuum, from its repressive forms to its discursive structures.

What conclusions are possible about the discourse of terrorism from the texts of the *Achille Lauro*/TWA incidents we have examined? And how might we use such an examination to improve our understanding of outbreaks of violence defined as "terrorism"? To be sure, the complicated drama(s) that developed following the incidents involved a complex interaction among the state, the media, the experts, and the public. The unfolding drama(s) played a central role in organizing and providing meaning to the incidents themselves and to a more general meaning of terrorism adopted by the state and mainstream society.

Terrorism and Future Analyses

The rhetoric following the *Achille Lauro*/TWA incidents suggests that terrorism is a term inextricably associated with and influenced by the political and the aesthetic. The control and expansion of moral, ideological, and/or political boundaries are expressed within specific discursive forms such as novels, media reports, scholarly reports, judicial transcripts, or illustrations. The term, terrorism, contains its own rhetoric, which has been transformed throughout history by different states. By claiming to be defining a certain type of violence, i.e., one that threatens the site of legitimate violence (the state), it is clear that this term is reserved for the art of statecraft. But do the terrorist scripts of experts, statespeople, media, or novelists typically include raped rainforests, starvation, abuse of children, or massacres of millions of people? Are these incidents not within the purview of the state? Are they not political or terrorist in nature?

In attempting to explain the art of statecraft, the construct of terrorism, and negotiation as a continuum process, we need to recognize that violence and discourse are two important interrelated components of this process. They are inevitably related, as the occurrence of one (either violence or discourse) is associated with the shaping of the "other." Examples which utilize terrorist rhetoric differently are common and obvious. In the United States, for example, George Washington is considered to be a revolutionary hero for illegally challenging, defeating, and purging the English state. Yet Gerry Adams, leader of Sinn Fein (IRA-related party), is viewed as a terrorist by the United States for suspected similar action. Less than a decade ago, Yasir Arafat was defined as a terrorist par excellence. Today he is viewed as a man of peace and condemns "terrorist" action.

Less obvious, however, are the cultural texts, narratives and, displays that have changed and been manipulated throughout history by different states. These texts and narratives are used in the discourses of academic and popular texts from schools, universities, private think tanks, religious organizations and rituals, legal documents, national anthems, folksongs, popular music, poetry, literature, and in public displays such as theme parks, community art centers, museums, heritage sites, and television. What is sorely lacking in contemporary research on terrorism are detailed examinations of how events, even ostensibly rare political events such as the *Achille Lauro* and TWA incidents, are propagated, diffused, and experienced in a particular culture, not as apt and isolated incidents but as narratives or stories. These stories are internalized, becoming part of a culture's collective memory, symbolism, morality, normative prescriptions as well as models for behavior. Viewed in this way, texts or cultural narratives are a dynamic and crucial process in the production of hegemony. For example, Robin Hood, Columbus sailing the ocean blue, the Boston Tea Party, the 47 Japanese samurai, the Spirit of Crazy Horse, and Zapata are not simple political events or "facts." These are historically complex events that have been authenticated by popular culture. Yet in the rush to make disciplinary generalizations, the histories of various cultures in the United States and around the world are seen as mere chronologies of political events, devoid of social context, that together or in isolation may "cause" another event (also motivated by politics or pathology). The insight that "terrorism is not a discrete topic that might be conveniently examined apart from the political, social and economic context in which it takes place . . . terrorism is a creature of its own time and place" (Cooper 1985, 95) paradoxically has been recognized superficially and denied substantively.

Furthermore, if terrorism is recognized within the discursive process of social construction, the nature of a society's political structures is re-presented. In some cases, as with the *Achille Lauro* incident in Italy, the discourse of the unfolding drama takes on the aspect of a competition among the numerous institutions and groups in society influencing the emergence of a "winning" viewpoint. In other cases, as with the TWA incident in the United States, the discursive forms are conceptualized in "either/or" terms from the start: either for or against, defining difference as danger to the state in all cases. Difference in this context is demonic, not diverse. This type of discursive structure reflects and shapes one dominant perspective, that of the state. Even those groups that claim to oppose the state are, in part, the embodiment and reflection of the state's repressive elements. So, when we define these groups as terrorist, we need to examine the source of this term, its foundation. If anything unnerving can be understood about "terrorism," it is this: its structural foundation is what makes it so impervious to its eradication. The state's involvement in supplying weapons, economic support, and refuge for perpetrators of violence not only exacerbates but perpetuates its repressive and violent essence.

The media's aesthetic involvement and influence in the TWA and *Achille Lauro* dramas also cannot be underestimated. They actively participated in perpetuating the notion of the state as accepting or rejecting cultural and political diversity. For the state to accept such diversity may involve risking its existence, as the Italian state did during the *Achille Lauro* incident. But while the Italian state is known for dismantling and rebuilding its own governments, its essence, which allows for this type of statecraft, remains the same. On the other hand, in the United States, the TWA incident did not allow for diverse interpretations. Does this mean that an ostensibly pluralistic society such as the U.S. is incapable of expressing multiple understandings upon the occurrence of a political incident? Perhaps. To be sure, if we look at the discourse of the unfolding drama of the TWA or any ostensible terrorist incident in the United States, we might conclude that the state has had one consistent response to it—one of repression despite the expression of multiple and diverse understandings.

While the United States is not devoid of alternative understandings, they are either effectively silenced, marginalized, sanitized, or swept aside, typically by the latest political fad. Incidents as recent as the bombings of American sites in Saudi Arabia, the Atlanta (Olympic village) bombing, or the TWA Flight 800 explosion spawned certain critical and provocative explanations. Ironically, the news media attempted to broadcast certain alternative explanations (such as the "friendly fire" theory for the TWA flight 800 explosion) but clearly defined them as "speculative," as well as casting doubt on their "reliability." Yet immediately following the flight 800 explosion, terrorism and possible "terrorist" targets were systematically defined and accused, though this information was also speculative. Indeed, the media spent a disproportionate amount of time defaming and denouncing the supposed "terrorist" suspected in the Olympic village bombing in Atlanta. The suspect was defined according to the typical reductionist pathology model: an alienated, disgruntled, vengeful personality. When the suspect was cleared months later, however, the media and most formal social control did nothing to repair this person's identity, or to publicize its investigation of other possible causes of the bombing or the dysfunctions of "intelligence" in either preventing the bombing or solving the mystery.

Adolph Hitler once boasted that if you tell a lie enough times, people will accept it as being the truth. In the 1400s it was heresy to proclaim that the world was round. The church blessed the killing of hundreds of thousands of "witches" despite its own belief in forgiveness. Today, the state and agencies re-presenting the state, such as the media and many supposed experts, continue to be involved in the anachronistic, patriarchal process of defining the terrorist, the "true" cause of increased state repression and social control. Clearly, this process suggests that truth is not other to the constructions of political rhetoric; thus, terrorism, as defined and reflected by the state, should not be viewed as a truth that is other to the constructions of political, aestheticized politics.

When we read what most experts have to say regarding terrorism, are we not to assume that terrorism has always meant the same thing over time and space? We are told that the terrorists come from a "culture of terrorism" and that U.S. citizens come from a culture of democracy and peace. We are supposed to view terrorism as a concept, with a predictable structure and parameters that we can scientifically understand and test rather than as a construct involved in the politics of statecraft.

Writers from Plato to Orwell have cautioned us about the processes by which history might repeat itself. Yet, the marketing of progress and civilization make it appear implausible that societies could repeat the horrors of the past. As we have examined the political production of statecraft involved in the production of truth, we can understand the process whereby the constructions of the past become dim memories. New generations inherit old problems and seek to redefine and/or discover new and improved solutions, yet one phenomenon remains consistent—that political discourse not only provides meaning to reality, but shapes our perceptions and responses to it—as with the construct of terrorism. Perhaps we would do well to study this process and attempt to understand it and explain it rather than claim to objectively know it.

Numerous books and articles have been written about terrorism, but how many of these recognize that they are a part of the narrow polemical construction of the term? How many admit to being involved in the productive politics of statecraft? C. Wright Mills (1959, 34) once noted that

> every self-conscious thinker must at all times be aware— and hence be able to control—the levels of abstraction on which he is working. The capacity to shuttle between levels of abstraction, with ease and with clarity is a signal mark of the imaginative and systematic thinker.

Many of the arguments suggested in this research directly challenge mainstream knowledge about terrorism, which in the last few decades has increasingly become complacent, stagnant, and dominated by ostensible experts threatened by or unable to think at different levels of analysis and degrees of abstraction (Lauderdale *et al.* 1990). As such, the analysis of terror, terrorists, and terrorism has been predominantly provided by a tiny fraction of the world's population residing primarily in privileged, yet estranged, spaces. It is time to reopen and reexamine these issues and present alternative questions and responses from the rest of humankind, people who also suffer daily from violence and terrorism.

AFTERWORD

Children still say, "Sticks and stones will break my bones, but words will never hurt me." Who created this cliche and by what processes? And what are we to make of similar fatuous ideas? Annamarie Oliverio has been told numerous times by colleagues that Italy is a country of anarchists or anarchism. She challenges this stereotype and other hegemonic concepts in her analysis of terrorism and terrorists. Her approach is compatible with recent work in the study of law and deviance that exposes the often invisible side of hegemonic social and political life. Scholars following her approach will note that words have a habit of jumping up from texts to direct and encourage the sticks and stones into action, sometimes under the label of "smart missiles."

One of the most important aspects of *The State of Terror* is its development of the term, hegemony. Numerous scholars use the term simply as a synonym for domination much as they throw in references to Foucault on power. Ironically, so did their ancestors in citing Parsons or Freud. This use is at once too narrow and too vacuous. *The State of Terror*, however, is not about reproducing fads or icons, or name-dropping. Oliverio's use of hegemony focuses upon the state's "war of position." Those who dominate modes of production, for example, impose and promote crucial world views through cultural means. These interpretations emerge from the control of central information sources, and ideas created by "objective" rulemakers are presented as unbiased. The media provide the most obvious example of this process, yet Oliverio also explicates the role of educators, health practitioners, and academics in producing meaning for the social world. As most of civil society assumes the dominant interpretive framework, individuals use the meanings and "truths" derived from their interpretations as standards by which to judge others. Alternative ideas suggested by those who criticize or do not follow the rules usually are dismissed as "biased," and in some instances individuals or groups in civil society are defined as deviants, e.g., sometimes as leaders and other times as terrorists.

Antonio Gramsci's concept of hegemony frames the problem of social life in a manner that is both general enough to account sociologically for the discursive processes of an advanced capitalist society and narrow enough to capture the contours of *in situ* behavior by individuals. Gramsci, the leader of the Italian Communist Party in the 1920s, was jailed in fascist prisons for his leadership. While in prison for ten years, Gramsci reconceived the concept of hegemony to explain the encompassing tactics of the fascists. Acknowledging the obvious role of political economy, he stressed the importance of understanding the manipulation of culture as a form of domination. Oliverio invokes hegemony in its Gramscian sense as a cultural concept rather than the typical misuse of Gramsci's concept as a solely political or economic idea.

Gramsci notes that hegemony is an order in which a certain way of life and thought is dominant, in which one world view permeates customs and political and religious ideas, especially their intellectual and moral connotations. In his analysis of hegemony, Gramsci draws the distinction between civil and political society. Civil society is characterized by private relations within private organizations, whereas political society is characterized by the state's use of coercive force to shape society so that it will conform to the mode of production. Gramsci conceives the war of position in terms of the role of the state in civil society. For Gramsci, a successful struggle for hegemony and collective will formation occurs within a general war of position. He compares two strategies for social change: the war of maneuver and the war of position. The war of maneuver comprised a strategy of a direct, typically violent and speedy confrontation between opposing principles. The 1848 revolutions in Europe and the Russian Revolution of 1917 were, for Gramsci, classic examples of wars of maneuver. Conversely, he understood the war of position as a slow, protracted struggle that involved diverse means which included "non-violent" aspects of civil society. For Gramsci, then, Gandhi's anti-colonialist resistance in India exemplifies a war of position.

Most importantly, however, Gramsci asks how individuals produce the material structures and objective conditions of social existence which appear before them as external forces and natural laws beyond their making or control. This is a question that has been examined by political theorist Richard Ashley and explicated here by Oliverio. The answer is to be found in the war of position: It is the practical struggle for hegemony, a struggle waged through intellectual and moral leadership leading to collective will formation. For a hegemonic order to survive, individuals must reproduce the practices and discourse that comprise the collective will. Interpretations of cause-effect relations, persons, places, and events that inform social practices and discourse must be similar to interpretations advanced by the practical and discursive elements of the social structure.

Information gleaned from our sensory experience is connected in a manner that simplifies understanding and recall. Sociologist Alfred Schutz suggests that "schemes of interpretation" provide people with frameworks for structuring and interpreting our experience. Psychologist Jean Piaget notes that we construct our world by assimilating it to schemas while accommodating these schemas to its constraints. And social psychologist Erving Goffman similarly notes that situations are defined "in accordance with principles of organization that govern events"; he calls these organizing structures "frames." Making sense of the external world requires scanning the environment, selecting features to attend to, and taking information about those features and either storing it for future retrieval or using it as a basis for action. A cognitive schema, then, serves as an interpretive mechanism that structures and assigns meaning to incoming information.

If individuals organize information in a schematic manner, we must understand how individuals develop one particular schema instead of another. That is, we must understand why certain features of the environment are attended to and acted upon while others are ignored or suppressed. Such an analysis requires us to examine the relationship between "schemes of interpretation" and social structures. We can actively pursue this research agenda by employing Oliverio's textual and contextual analysis. To understand how "schemes of interpretation" are connected with social structures, we must understand:

1. the social organization that permits the definers of social "reality" to do their defining
2. the relationship between power and the mechanism by which information is disseminated
3. the relationship between social information and constructions of reality.

Oliverio suggests that these processes can be explored using Foucault's work on power and knowledge. Power is intimately connected with knowledge. Those who generate and control knowledge are often perceived to speak the truth. "'Truth' is linked in a circular relation with systems of power which produce and sustain it, and to effects of power which it induces and which extend it—A 'regime' of truth." Stories of ostensible truth become deeply problematic. Which story, for example, do we believe about the Zapatistas in Chiapas?

The construction of a story is crucial to the production of hegemony and "reality" because it represents only selected features of what individuals and a society experience. Narratives may produce "reality" by interpreting and explaining selectively a set of experiences and by teaching what is expected of everyone in light of that "reality." Stories situate everyone, allowing them to understand where they are in an otherwise incomprehensible sea of facts and events. In so doing, stories give meaning and coherence to what would otherwise be confusing or random phenomena.

One story dominating Western society is that it must have a preponderance of modern criminal law. The expansion of criminal law and punishment occurred primarily as a consequence of the growth of centralized state control and its emphasis on efficiency via hierarchy and elitism. Proponents of punishment through criminal law focused initially on indigenous people or those disadvantaged by income, gender, race, or ethnicity. And, as Oliverio cogently notes, this focus continues unabated. In the United States, for example, the state now also reserves some of the severest penalties for whoever is defined as a terrorist.

The emphasis on the punitive powers of the state at the expense of the restitutive rights of victims provides an exploitative device to maintain political power and derive pecuniary benefits. The type of argument usually articulated in defense of the modern system of punishment is to deter future similar wrongdoings and to educate the community. The criminal act, therefore, becomes the occasion but not necessarily the reason for ceremonial punitive measures. In this light, whether the state's emphasis is on physically punishing, rehabilitating, or imprisoning the offender, the actual levying of punishment is not done for the sake of the offender, but for political purposes. The state does not involve the victim in the justice process other than to satisfy feelings of revenge, which are insignificant compared to the further legitimation of the status quo. On the other hand, stories attempting to bring about equality and social justice directed to underlying transformations in society and the world system typically are ignored or viewed as fantasy.

Another story often ignored is that civil action and law were the foundation of most indigenous cultures, despite modern claims that civil law emerged from recent civilization. Yet, in North America, anthropologists and archaeologists have not found evidence of prisons prior to colonization. American Indian Phillip Deere asks: "How did different Nations of people speaking so many different languages live without these institutions?" Civil law, based on traditional American Indian procedures, has the potential to provide a more equitable, less oppressive arena in which to negotiate and regulate major social problems, including those of a violent nature. Civil proceedings carry far less degradation to the parties involved and de-emphasize the moral condemnation or stigma of criminal sanctions. Civil sanctions are alternatives to repressive punishments for both the specific parties involved and the broader system of law and justice. However, civil alternatives typically are suffocated before they reach any public policy agenda.

The secular nature of dominant analyses of law often justifies law's existence upon religious grounds, albeit with passing references to economic concerns. In this respect, it might be wise to consult the Apostle Paul as he spoke to the Galatians about the "curse of the law" for Jews and Gentiles.

In this respect, *The State of Terror* is important in reminding us that when justice is reduced to a juridical concept it is only of derivative interest. The valuable research in this area actually focuses upon injustice studied within particular historical and comparative contexts. One especially relevant perspective investigates how institutionalized rules take the form of cultural theories, ideologies, and prescriptions about how society actually operates in contrast to how it should work to attain collective purposes, in particular, goals of justice and progress.

Oliverio's analysis of the modern state is cogent, especially in regard to violence when it is defined as terrorism. Some militia movements in the United States, for example, are similar to the state they deplore in their mutual reliance upon violence. If the state teaches that violence is a legitimate means to resolve problems then others may resort to it when reason fails and force prevails. More importantly, Oliverio's theoretical approach, her textual and contextual analysis, provides a framework for revealing much more complex relationships.

We have been told by the media in the United States that Italy is full of anarchy, anarchists, and terrorists and that the United States is full of law, lawyers, and stability. What we hear or read is often not what we see. Indeed, the whole world may be watching. In the United States we recently observed the rocky rapids of Whitewater following Iran-Contragate and Watergate, and the controversies surrounding Waco, Ruby Ridge, the Unabomber, and the Freemen. In the state of Arizona we saw the indictment of Governor Symington following the impeachment of Governor Mecham. In Oklahoma City we watched the Federal building explosion, and in Comanche County, Oklahoma, we experience the terror felt by indigenous people who are treated as non-persons, even non-Indians, if their mix of Indian blood does not meet the Bureau of Indian Affairs (often termed Bossing Indians Around) standards. Oliverio suggests that the development of the state can lead to social structures that are conducive to varied forms of terror. We remember the assassinations of John F. Kennedy, Robert Kennedy, and Martin Luther King, and the numerous attempts to assassinate American Indian leader Russell Means. As these previously invisible events become visible, they crack the hegemonic facade of stability. And the politics of deviance and the rhetoric of terrorism become more obvious.

Among other things, this book takes a major step in transforming the study of law and deviance into the study of social harm. Scholars also would be wise to use Oliverio's framework to pursue a new field of jurisprudence. Law as the weapon of the state desperately needs attention, especially in light of the internationalization and globalization of culture. *The State of Terror* suggests that state terrorism is fragmented war and such war is ubiquitous. But who is willing to recognize it?

Pat Lauderdale

NOTES

1. Prologue

1. Within weeks after the arrest of the alleged Unabomber in April 1996, texts emerged for popular reading, such as Douglas and Olshaker's *Unabomber* (1996, Pocket Books), providing a meaning and reality to a virtually unknown and undefined series of events from the preceding twenty years. Such texts glorify an otherwise futile twenty-year FBI investigation and sensationalize the "hermit" or deviant lifestyle of the alleged terrorist, providing a cause (via motivation and/or socialization) for his action.

2. The seventies in Italy saw the rise of the Communist Party and more radical "communist" groups with which the Party wanted to dissociate itself. The Red Brigades was but one of these groups and they were defined as the "real" terrorists, the real cause of instability in the Italian nation-state. The nineties often is being re-presented as the rise of fascism once again in Italy. Only this time, the fascists are being elected via the democratic process rather than via a *coup d'état*. The sites of their electoral victories have been in the south. Instead of terrorism, the mafia is blamed for destabilizing the state. Radical fascist groups, while engaging in violent action, are not being defined as "terrorists." Paradoxically, popular Italian historical accounts always emphasize how the only time in Italian history in which the mafia was effectively suppressed was during the Fascist era from 1919 to 1943 (on this latter point, see Chubb 1989).

3. The Red Brigades espoused what were considered to be Marxist-Leninist principles. They were generally defined as a "leftist" organization, as was the Communist Party. Whenever a bombing or kidnapping took place, even though there were supposedly 297 other so-called leftist organizations, all attempting to claim responsibility for the attacks (not to mention the sixty-four supposedly rightist organizations), the blame always managed to rest with the Red Brigades (Pisano 1987).

4. Consider, for example, the distinction President Clinton makes between what he refers to as unorthodox, legal protest and terrorist violence:

> They have a right to believe whatever they want, they have a right to say whatever they want, they have a right to keep and bear arms, they have a right to put on uniforms and go out on the weekends. . . . They do not have the right to kill innocent Americans. They do not have the right to violate the laws. And they do not have the right to take the position that if somebody comes to arrest them for violating the law they're perfectly justified in killing them. They are wrong in that. (Raum 1995, 4)

Yet, the distinction between unorthodox, legal protest and terrorist violence becomes ambiguous when applied to specific individuals or groups (see the cases of Leonard Peltier, Angela Davis, Bobby Seale, or the Black Panthers, and the American Indian movement).

5. For a detailed explanation of this process, see Lauderdale, McLaughlin, and Oliverio, "Levels of Analysis, Theoretical Orientations and Degrees of Abstraction," in *The American Sociologist* 21 (1990):29–40.

6. In analyzing the discourse of terrorism, there are a number of different routes or disciplines that may be followed, such as anthropology, linguistics, philosophy; however, none of these disciplines stand alone in the rhetoric of the theater. The rhetoric and organizing framework of the theater cut across all these various disciplines. As a result, the theater metaphor has the virtue of inviting us to ask many of the questions posed in these other fields.

7. Italian is my first language, and I also studied the Italian language and literature at the Scuola di Piazza Card. S. Niccolo, in Prato, Italy.

2. Writing the Script: Language, Hegemony, and Historical Interpretation

1. Kuhn (1970) explains how scientists expected to observe certain effects by utilizing their theoretical perspectives and scientific instruments. Scientific anomalies were often ignored until the discovery of a new scientific paradigm, and then those anomalies became

part of the argument proposing the need for a new paradigm. The scientific anomalies discussed by Kuhn were the product of specific ways of explaining or describing reality.

2. For a discussion of dominator-type societies, see Eisler (1987). She argues that the central issue in understanding the inadequacy of contemporary societies to provide justice, equity and, peace lies within their dominator-type social structures. Terrorist activity, from this perspective, occurs as a result of the relations of domination produced in such structures.

3. See Frank's (1993) argument that economic development has been continuing for 5000 years, and the extended set of responses to his argument by leading scholars in that area.

4. Social differentiation and rationalization are also significant nineteenth-century references. While it is beyond the immediate scope of this inquiry to explicate the legacy of these theoretical conceptions in the contemporary construct of terrorism, the field or discipline of terrorism has produced an interesting rationalization of expertise, each specializing in knowledge about a different aspect of the phenomenon. For recent examples of this process of knowledge rationalization in terrorism, see Stohl (1988) and Moxon-Brown (1994).

5. Yet the reasoning rarely is detached and the logical arguments are couched in extremely narrow renderings of Aristotelian logic. Moreover, there is little systematic theory with clear distinctions among definitions, assumptions, and hypotheses. And the interpretations of the empirical data typically claim that their theory is correct, rather than in a state of confirmation or disconfirmation.

6. For an important examination of the process of statemaking and its similarity to other rhetorical structures of violence and their prescriptive implications, see Tilly (1985, 169–191).

3. Setting the Stage: Foundations of Meaning for Terrorism

1. After the Risorgimento, literacy increasingly came under the control of the state in Italy, just as the spread of literacy during the eighteenth and nineteenth centuries did in the United States. Nancy Armstrong (1985, 2) suggests that "Enlightenment discourse took up the project of decentralizing political authority by giving each individ-

ual sovereignty over himself and his property." Literacy was brought under the control of the state "through a broadening of the university curriculum, through a series of school reforms, as well as through the creation of libraries, reviews, journals, encyclopedias, vernacular dictionaries, grammars and a variety of still more subtle instruments of regulation, among which one must include the family itself." This process of creating the nation and its citizens reached an unprecedented level during the Fascist era in Italy and while the spread of literacy and concurrent economic development (especially of the "backward" rural south) was celebrated, the forms of literacy that were suppressed were not considered until recently (cf. Gramsci 1966).

2. During the Fascist era, themes of pageantry, nationalism, obedience and respect for authority were essential and enforced in many ways by the regime (cf. Geertz 1981). One of the ways obedience and respect were reinforced both directly and indirectly was through the language. The formal pronouns in Italian are typically in the third person singular and plural. Under Fascism, this was changed to the second person plural for all cases. While the familiar pronouns are most commonly used in Italy today, under Fascism it was customary to use the impersonal pronoun *voi*, even with family members.

3. It was not until 1976 that in Italy a law (no. 202) was passed allowing for privately owned channels and stations to operate at local levels. Until then, the RAI corporation (Radio Audizione Italiana), the national public corporation of radio and television had complete control.

4. In Verona, for example, various theater productions are staged outdoors, in the streets, in the park, or wherever appropriate for the plot. The audience actively participates in the production. Even appropriate weather conditions are important. For example, if rain is needed, the audience will wait for the rain—even if they have to return at some other time to continue the production. As one might expect, such theater productions can last for days. Tourists come from everywhere to experience the theater in Verona.

5. There are certain literary exceptions to this, of course. Some cultural artifacts in the form of science fiction or adventure/action do not always conform to a linear, chronological structure. However, they are defined as "alternative" forms of literature and are not typically viewed as re-presenting "normal," everyday reality. If anything, these forms are typically contrasted to "reality."

6. The new Holocaust Museum in Washington, D.C., can be examined in the way that Goldberg (1993) views the museums (mis)representing indigenous life in South Africa.

7. Also, see Oliverio and Lauderdale 1996; Brown and Merrill 1993.

8. "The King's" or "Queen's English" is a phrase commonly used to represent the official, hence proper, form of English. Even though certain standard English forms in the United States deviate from standard English in Great Britain, we nonetheless hear or read our information in what is considered to be the official form of the language, certainly not in any southern dialect. Nor do news media personages, as different as they may be individually (i.e., Connie Chung and Geraldo Rivera), have any strikingly noticeable accents. Dialects and accents and even individual "flair" are most often viewed as "deviations" from appropriate writing standards. The appropriate writing standard, typified by what we read in most newspapers, magazines, journals, books, and government reports and/or hear on any news show, reflects and conforms to a certain sameness of interpretive form and practice, even though the interpreters themselves may be very different.

9. The recent massacre of Lebanese civilians by Israeli artillery provides an explicit example of this process whereby the "winners" produce history. The U.N. declared the incident as a "deliberate" act, Israel claimed it was a "mistake." In south Lebanon, Israel supports an army they call "the army of south Lebanon (in Hebrew: Tzadal). It is headed by a Lebanese general giving the impression of a state-sponsored, "legitimate" army. Foreign press calls this "an army of mercenaries." Israel refers to Hizbullah's people as "terrorists," while the foreign press refers to them as "guerrilla" (Ben-Yehuda, 1996: personal correspondence).

4. (Re)Constructing the Event: The *Achille Lauro* Plot

1. Apparently, there were also about fifty Swiss, thirty Austrians, and ten Germans; however, it is interesting to note that different estimates were given in different reports. In Italy, each text examined varied from the others not only on how many people were on board but also how it was presented. For example, sometimes the passengers

that got off in Alexandria and were going to meet the rest of the passengers at Port Said were included in the estimate, sometimes not.

2. The words "incident" and "event" are used for clarity, an obvious re-presentation, as the *Achille Lauro* is also the name of a ship and TWA an airline corporation.

3. Such corruption consisting of government connections with the mafia, as well as corporate corruption such as kickback schemes, have existed in Italy for a long time. And, more importantly, people always openly spoke about these features of the Italian state. However, what changed in the 1990s regarding these features is that they suddenly became recognized publicly as the leading social problem of the day. Whereas before people knew about it but just took it for granted, in recent years the media were filled with dramatic reports of various high-ranking political officials (including the former prime minister involved in the *Achille Lauro* incident, Craxi) being dragged off to prison for their clandestine connection to the mafia. Today, the *real* threat to the essence and "stability" of the Italian state is identified as being its life-long tragic struggle with the mafia and corporate corruption.

4. The suggestion that terrorism is at present the focus of discursive struggle in the United States can be seen quite easily in texts reporting "world" news. The words, terror or terrorism, are consistently used to depict how this sort of action occurs regularly in "other" nation-states, nation-states we may view as deviant. Terrorism is characteristic of inherently deviant nations, nations we may consider our enemies at any convenient political time.

5. Wagner-Pacifici (1986) discusses how talk shows such as David Hartman's were used to display the hostages (and the terrorists) of the TWA incident. Even though it was a blatant melodramatic display of innocence versus maliciousness, she maintains that the Americans are more skilled than the Italians at maintaining that there is nothing selective or aesthetically crafted about such political presentations (cf. Benjamin 1969). If any identity formation occurs between protagonists and audiences, it is between the hostages or victims and the audience. Any display of ambiguity by the hostages (e.g., the so-called Stockholm Syndrome) (cf. Stohl 1988) is viewed as a "tragedy" caused by the evil, manipulative terrorist.

6. Currently in Italy the existing political parties have aligned themselves according to two different ideological party positions: Cen-

tro Sinistra (left of center) and Centro Destra (right of center). This means that the previously dominant Christian Democratic Party has split between the two ideological directions. The Centro Sinistra party is called "L'ulivo" and headed by Prodi, and Centro Destra is called "il Polo della Liberta" headed by Berlusconi. Currently, Prodi is the head of government in Italy.

5. (Re)Constructing the Event: The Hijacking of TWA 847

1. The dominance of the medical model in contemporary U.S. society has much to do with the attitude that all problems can be or should be fixed and resolved. Treating the problem, rather than diagnosing it more precisely, is the predominant trend of the medical model (Oliverio and Lauderdale 1996). It gives the impression that something is being done. This treatment focus is especially obvious when U.S. medical research is compared to the research emerging from various European societies. Conrad and Schneider (1980, 35), in providing a political analysis of the medicalization of deviance, note that in 1851 a physician named Samuel Cartwright discussed the "disease" known as "drapetomania." It apparently only affected slaves and its major symptom included running away from the white masters' plantations. Less than a decade later, slavery itself was proclaimed a crime according to the Fourteenth Ammendment (cf. Lauderdale 1980). The state and its expansion into the therapeutic realm, with its millions of employees in "human services," has adopted this medical model for ostensibly resolving problems both virtually as well as figuratively. The state can more easily appear to do something, to take care of its people (Polsky 1991).

2. Although most feminist writers (or other writers who claim to be representing the voices of the oppressed) have not explicitly made this connection, terrorism may be examined as a practice of domination, a practice characteristic of dominator-type societies, where power and politics are viewed and practiced in Machiavellian terms—to gain advantage (cf. Brown and Merrill 1993; Eisler 1987; Foucault 1979).

3. In *Discipline and Punish*, Foucault (1979) discusses this disciplinary ideal and how it relates to normalizing judgments and professions, discourse and power. Briefly, the disciplinary ideal refers to the limiting, directing, and controlling of human will. For example, fields of study such as philosophy, history, literature remain confined within

their specific poles of argumentation. Within the fields, they are unable to question their inherent boundaries, nor are they able to communicate successfully with one another. Such self-enclosure allows for the emergence of competing, contradictory, or unrelated truths to appear as a coherent field, discipline, or discourse. The discourse emerging from these abstract classifications "differentiates the 'text' from the 'context' where it had a political role to play. This endows language with a false innocence or sincerity" (See Armstrong 1985, 4). Foucault refers to this type of knowledge production through different fields of study as "normalizing" professions. Each "profession" presumes a certain normalized order of things that is inherent in society. Knowledge produced in these professions is an exercise of power and it defines, limits, and regulates will. The inherent assumption of the normalized order presented is that there is no need for visible violence, and in instances where the mere exercise of knowledge is not enough, such as with terrorism, the site of visible violence, the state, exercises its power to restore reason, truth, and knowledge. Foucault in his analysis, therefore, collapses history together with power and discourse suggesting that the world is no less violent for exercising power through language rather than through physical force if language indeed provides the agent of hegemony (see also Lacan 1966 and Derrida 1976).

4. In accordance with Foucault's "archaeology," this study also "dismisses a unitary conception of truth and with that, the notion that a progressive accumulation of information leads to 'knowledge'" (rather than simply "order") (see Ericson, Baranek, and Chan 1991; Pudaloff 1985).

5. McLoughlin (1978) provides a very lucid account of the various eras of religious revitalizations and awakenings in the United States, which accompanied underlying economic and social transformations. His text is replete with descriptions of American religious fundamentalists who have profiles that can match or rival contemporary profiles of "terrorists" that predominate. They used their religious fundamentalism to justify the almost complete elimination of the many indigenous nations—not to mention the fact that many of these "Puritans" are celebrated as providing American Independence (by using "terrorist" tactics) from the legitimate sovereign at the time—Great Britain.

6. The lyrics to "The Star Spangled Banner" reify U.S. pride in the defeat of the British state in 1777, although the lyrics specifically refer

to an unsuccessful bombing of an American fort by the British in 1812. The leaders of the colonies seeking independence were viewed as "terrorist" by the colonists in 1777. But by 1812, the U.S. republic viewed the British bombing as "terrorist," and France supported the former's declaration of war against the latter.

7. See Lauderdale (1980, 4–7), on the dichotomous distinction made in most sociological research between political and apolitical deviants and the implications for a society's response to each category. See also Ben-Yehuda (1990, 3–4), for a discussion of political deviance and political elements in "regular" deviance.

8. The publication of the Unabomber's manifesto provides a recent example of this controversy surrounding what the media should or should not print for political reasons, rather than as a concern for just reporting the facts.

9. More recently, Arafat has been reported as condemning the Oklahoma bombing action. This condemnation occurred when the suspects of the bombing were still considered to be Palestinians.

10. While having more "time" is almost redundantly used as a reason for the success of the *Achille Lauro* event compared to the failure of the TWA event (Rubin 1986), "time" could have produced different consequences. The ostensible terrorists could have had enough time to systematically destroy 600 people as has occurred in other incidents, i.e., 1972 Olympic games in Munich, Jim Jones in Guyana, Iranian hostages, Koresh in Waco. A lot of time is not necessarily a factor that leads to success.

11. There have been times, however, when a certain amount of ambiguity has slipped through the cracks of the media's tunnel vision of reality, and this has led to a very different response on the part of public opinion toward the whole issue of terrorism. However, this sense of ambiguity was portrayed more clearly by the Italian media sources (as in the *Achille Lauro* case) than the U.S. media sources in either the TWA or in other incidents more generally.

6. Props, Sets, Stunts: The Global Transmission of Reality

1. Texts generated and distributed via the Internet system have not only increased the "pace" and number of texts circulating, but also

further reduced the "space" from where these texts come. The fast-paced, short vignette that does not necessarily follow any linear narrative mode and is received from anywhere in the world in a matter of minutes best exemplifies this system of computerized communication (Der Derian 1987).

2. Spanish film director Luis Bunuel once said that his films contained a beginning, middle, and end, but not necessarily in that order. His statement has become a popular reality for other film makers, theater playwrights, and, of course, writers.

3. I have replaced the common term "traditional" values with "hegemonic" values. The word, traditional, presumes that those values have existed for all time, and that present conditions in the world are aberrations. As aberrations, the assumption is that contemporary values and conditions will come to pass. Yet what is re-presented as traditional refers to a relatively brief hegemony in time and space.

4. The indigenous revolt in Chiapas is an example of how references to terrorism to describe this action have led to misunderstandings of the people and their society. According to Esteva (1994, 85), this indigenous movement is comprised of "networks of groups—coalitions of discontent which share certain characteristics: they are deliberately open and allow for the participation of different ideologies and classes; they consciously avoid any temptation to lead or control the social forces they activate; they opt instead for flexible organizational structures, which they use for concerted action, rather than for channelling demands; they explicitly detach themselves from abstract ideologies, preferring to concentrate on specific campaigns (for example, against a dam, a road, a nuclear plant or the violations of human rights); and they exhaust any democratic means and legal procedures available before resorting to direct action or revolt."

5. Traditionally in most sociological research, a distinction is made between "political" and "apolitical" deviance (cf. Merton 1968). While the former is viewed as challenging the legitimacy of rules and laws for the sake of a higher moral cause, the latter is viewed as accepting the existing order, but attempting to avoid it for personal, selfish gain. While this dichotomy has provided a useful point of analytical departure, some sociologists have explained its limited utility and view all forms of deviance as inherently political and rhetorically amenable (Lauderdale and Oliverio 1995; Ben-Yehuda 1990; Laud-

erdale 1980). This position is more theoretically heuristic for understanding the social construction of deviance and for understanding the social construction of terrorism.

7. Terrorism: The Art of Statecraft

1. For a detailed account of this series of events, including the tangenti scandals and the return of the mafia, as the leading destabilizing threat to Italian democracy, see Grundle and Parker (1996). It is important to note that the emergence of the mafia has been described as a product of the abolition of the Italian feudal system, the introduction of the market system and modern state into the Southern Italian countryside, even though the mafia's patrimonial structure is reflective of feudal political organization. The abolition of the Italian feudal system began formally in 1812, but continued informally well into the twentieth century (Chubb, 1989). Franchetti and Sonnino (1974: 72) noted that "both wealth and the capacity to prevail through violence became accessible to a larger number of people, and the ruffians, who before had been in the employ of the barons, became independent; thus to obtain their services, they now had to be dealt with as equals" (cf. Inverarity *et al.* 1983, 72–87).

2. Indeed, most Italians are not fundamentally threatened by the "instability" of the government. They often view "stable" democracies as authoritarian democracy. Inasmuch as Italian citizens are critical of their governmental situation, they are also proud of the fact that under conditions of supposed corruption, scandal, or other mishandlings, the government is instantly dissolved and a new one is formed.

3. As I mentioned in the first chapter, the historical context for this almost transcendent public perception and understanding of terrorism has evolved over time. While the competitive practice of politics and power may be evidenced in previous terrorist incidents such as the Moro affair, as a site of discursive struggle, terrorism appears to have seen its twilight in Italy. The current destabilizing influences are defined as the mafia and government corruption (Grundle and Parker 1996; Chubb 1989).

4. The return of the hijacked Boeing airliner and the offensive strategy employed by the Reagan administration were greeted by the public with such jubilation that one of Reagan's officials was quoted as

considering the event as a "God-given opportunity" for raising national morale. Such is the essence of ritual/spectacles that reinforce and praise the ultimate victory of good over evil (Cassese 1989).

8. Epilogue

1. The state, and its various manifestations, has been the focus of analysis for numerous scholars since Socrates. It is neither the purpose nor the scope of this book to pay homaage to all these treatises as they may or may not relate to terrorism. The book specifically refers to the intellectual descendancy of the construct of terrorism (as it is understood in contemporary society) and certain views of the state, such as Gramsci's and Foucault's, that provide important points of departure for the analysis of terrorism in the art of statecraft.

2. Domestic abuse is obviously very complex. There may be the intent to inflict harm, which leads to abuse; however, there may be no intention to inflict harm, which still leads to a violent consequence, what has been termed as "accidental" violence. Regardless of the intent, abusive consequences create terror.

3. The issue of whether or not it is appropriate to define and/or conceptualize domestic violence as terrorism is less problematic when it is examined in terms of different levels of analysis and degrees of abstraction. For a detailed explication of this approach to understanding the fundamental and substantive links to what appear to be various types of social research, see Lauderdale *et al.* (1990).

REFERENCES

Alberoni, Francesco. December 1985. "Due Strategie e Due Metodi Contrapposti: Armi o Diplomazia Contro il Terrorismo?" *Corriere della Sera*. Milano: 1.

Allen, Paula Gunn. 1986. *The Sacred Hoop*. Boston: Beacon Press.

Allison, Alexander W., Arthur J. Carrand, and Arthur M. Eastman. 1979. *Masterpieces of the Drama*. New York: MacMillan Publishing Co.

Anderson, Benedict. 1983. *Imagined Communities: Reflections on the Origin and Spread of Nationalism*. London: Verso.

Antonio, Robert J. 1995. "Nietzsche's Antisociology: Subjectified Culture and the end of History." *American Journal of Sociology* 101: 1–43.

Arendt, Hannah. 1969. *On Violence*. New York: Harcourt Brace Jovanovich.

Armstrong, Nancy. 1985. "Introduction." *Semiotica* 54: 1–9.

Artaud, Antonin. 1958. *The Theater and its Double*. New York: Calder and Boyars.

Ashley, Richard K. (Unpublished Manuscript, 1984). "Theory as War: Antonio Gramsci and the War of Position." Arizona State University.

———, and R. B. J. Walker. 1990. "Speaking the Language of Exile: Dissident Thought in International Studies." *International Studies Quarterly* 34: 259–268.

Augelli, Enrico, and Craig Murphy. 1988. *America's Quest for Supremacy and the Third World: A Gramscian Analysis*. London: Pinter Publishers.

Avalle, Silvio D. 1970. *L'analisi Letteraria in Italia: Formalismo, Strutturalismo, Semiologia*. Milano-Napoli: R. Ricciardi.

Bachrach, Peter, and Morton Baratz. 1970. *Power and Poverty*. New York: Oxford University Press.

Banfield, Edward. 1958. *The Moral Basis of a Backward Society*. London: Printers.

Barthes, Roland. 1977. *Image, Music, Text*. New York: Hill and Wang.

Baudrillard, Jean. 1983a. *Simulations*. New York: Semiotext(e).

————. 1983b. *Le Strategie Fatali*. Milan: Feltrinelli.

Bechelloni, Giovanni. 1984. *L'immaginario Quotidiano*. Torino: ERI.

Becker, Howard S. (1963) 1973. *Outsiders: Studies in the Sociology of Deviance*. New York: Free Press.

Bell, Bowyer J. 1974. *The Secret Army: A History of the IRA 1916–1970*. Cambridge: MIT Press.

————. 1978. *A Time of Terror: How Democratic Societies Respond to Revolutionary Violence*. NewYork: Basic Books.

————. 1994. "The Armed Struggle and Underground Intelligence: An Overview." *Studies in Conflict and Terrorism* 17: 115–150.

Benjamin, Walter. 1969. "The Work of Art in the Age of Mechanical Reproduction." P. 65 in *Illuminations*, edited by H. Arendt. New York: Schocken Books.

Bentley, Eric. 1968. *The Theory of the Modern Stage*. New York: Penguin Books.

Ben-Yehuda, Nachman. 1990. *The Politics and Morality of Deviance*. Albany: SUNY Press.

————. 1993. *Political Assassinations by Jews: A Rhetorical Device for Justice*. Albany: SUNY Press.

————. Forthcoming, 1997. "Political Assassination Events As a Form of Alternative Justice." *International Journal of Contemporary Sociology*.

Bobbio, Norberto. 1983. "Italy's Permanent Crisis," *Telos* 54: 123–133.

Bondanella, Peter, and Mark Musa. 1979. *The Portable Machiavelli*. New York: Penguin Books.

Boyer, Paul, and Stephen Nissenbaum. 1974. *Salem Possessed: The Social Origins of Witchcraft*. Cambridge: Harvard University Press.

Brown, David J., and Robert Merrill, eds. 1993. *Violent Persuasions: The Politics and Imagery of Terrorism*. Seattle: Bay Press.

Brown, William, J. 1990. "The Persuasive Appeal of Mediated Terrorism: The Case of the TWA Flight 847 Hijacking," *Western Journal of Speech Communication* 54: 219–236.

Burke, Edmund. [1790] 1969. *Reflections on the Revolution in France*. Edited by C.C. O'Brien. London: Penguin.

Caldwell, Leslie. 1986. "Reproducers of the Nation: Women and the Family in Fascist Policy," Pp. 110–141 in *Rethinking Italian Fascism*, edited by David Forgacs. London: Lawrence and Wishart.

Cassese, Antonio. 1989. *Terrorism, Politics and Law: The Achille Lauro Affair*. Cambridge: Basil Blackwell.

Cetron, Marvin J. 1989. "The Growing Threat of Terrorism," *The Futurist* 23(4): 20–24.

Chaze, W.L. 1985. "Reagan's Hostage Crisis." *U.S. News and World Report* 99(1) (July 8): 18–21.

Cherry, Conrad. 1971. *God's New Israel*. Scarborough, Ontario: Prentice Hall.

Chomsky, Noam. 1959. "On Certain Formal Properties of Grammars." *Information and Control* 2: 137–167.

——— . 1987. "International Terrorism: Image and Reality." *Crime and Social Justice* 27–28: 172–200.

Chubb, Judith. 1989. *The Mafia and Politics: The Italian State Under Siege*. Cornell University: Center for International Studies.

Clark, Ramsey. 1993. "Beyond Terrorism." Pp. 67–86 in *Violent Persuasions: The Politics and Imagery of Terrorism*, edited by David Brown and Robert Merrill. Seattle: Bay Press.

Clastres, Pierre. 1977. *Society Against the State*. New York: Urizen Books.

Colella, Ugo. (Unpublished Manuscript, 1989). *Alienation and the Story of the Story*. Stanford University.

Commager, Henry S. 1985. "Nations Aren't Innocent," *New York Times* (June 27), 22.

Connell, R.W. 1985. "Theorizing Gender." *Sociology* 19: 260–272.

Conrad, Peter, and Joseph W. Schneider. 1980. *Deviance and Medicalization*. St. Louis: C.V. Mosby Co.

Cooper, H.H.A. 1978. "Terrorism and the Intelligence Function." Pp. 287–296 in *International Terrorism in the Living World*, edited by M.H. Livingston. Westport, Conn.: Greenwood Press.

Corrado, Raymond. 1981. "A Critique of the Mental Disorder Perspective of Political Terrorism." *International Journal of Law and Psychiatry* 4: 1–47.

———. 1988. "Ethnic and Ideological Terrorism in Western Europe." Pp. 373–344 in *The Politics of Terrorism*, edited by Michael Stohl. New York: Marcel Dekker, Inc.

Court of Assize of Genoa. Unpublished Text. Decision of 10 July, 1986, filed with the Registrar on 27 December, 1986.

Crelinsten, Ronald D., and Alex P. Schmid. 1995. *The Politics of Pain*. San Francisco: Westview Press.

Crenshaw, Martha. 1979.*Revolutionary Terrorism*. Stanford: Hoover Institution.

———. 1983. *Terrorism, Legitimacy and Power: The Consequences of Political Violence*. Middletown, Conn.: Wesleyan University Press.

———, ed. 1995. *Terrorism in Context*. University Park: Pennsylvania State Press.

Crozier, Brian. 1960. *The Rebels*. Boston: Beacon Press.

———. 1978. "U.S. Senate Subcommittee on Internal Security." P. 3 in *Political Terrorism*, edited by L.A. Sobel. Oxford: Clio.

della Porta, Donatella. 1995. "Left-Wing Terrorism in Italy." Pp. 105–159 in *Terrorism in Context*, edited by Martha Crenshaw. University Park: Pennsylvania State Press.

deLauretis, Teresa. 1985. "The Violence of Rhetoric: Considerations on Representation and Gender." *Semiotica* 54(1/2): 11–31.

Deloria, Vine. (1973) 1992. *God is Red*. Grosset and Dunlap.

Demerath, Nicholas J., and Phillip E. Hammond. 1969. *Religion in Social Context: Tradition and Transition*. New York: Random House.

Deming, A. 1985. "Lebanon's Holy Warriors," *Newsweek*, 106(1) (July 1): 25–26.

Department of State Bulletin. 1985. Interview with the Legal Adviser to the State Department, M.A.D. Sofaer, pp. 79–80.

Der Derian, James. 1987. *On Diplomacy: A Genealogy of Western Estrangement*. Oxford: Basil Blackwell.

————. 1990. "The (S)pace of International Relations." *International Studies Quarterly* 34(3): 295–310.

Derrida, Jacques. 1976. *Of Grammatology*, translated by Gayatri Spivak. Baltimore: Johns Hopkins University Press.

De Rosa, Gerardi. 1987. "Una Crisi di Governo Imprevista." *Cronaca Contemporanea* 30: 383–391.

Dinnerstein, Leonard, and David M. Reimers. 1988. *Ethnic Americans*. New York: Harper and Row.

Di Palma, Giuseppe. 1977. *Surviving Without Governing: The Italian Parties in Parliament*. Berkeley: University of California Press.

Douglas, John, and Mark Olshaker. 1996. *Unabomber*. New York: Pocket Books.

Drake, Robert. 1989. *The Revolutionary Mystique and Terrorism in Contemporary Italy*. Bloomington: Indiana University Press.

————. 1995. *The Aldo Moro Murder Case*. Cambridge: Harvard University Press.

Ducibella, Joseph W. 1969. *The Phonology of the Sicilian Dialects*. New York: AMS Press.

Durkheim, Emile. (1912) 1948. *The Elementary Forms of the Religious Life*. Glencoe, Ill.: Free Press.

Duvall, Raymond D., and Michael Stohl. 1988. "Governance by Terror." Pp. 231–272 in *The Politics of Terrorism*, edited by M. Stohl. New York: Marcel Dekker, Inc.

Ebenstein, William. 1969. *Great Political Thinkers*. New York: W.W. Norton.

Eco,Umberto. 1979. *The Role of the Reader: Explorations in the Semiotics of Texts*. Bloomington: Indiana University Press.

Eisler, Rianne. 1987. *The Chalice and the Blade*. New York: Harper Collins.

Ericson, Richard V., Patricia M. Baranek, and Janet B.L. Chan. 1987. *Visualizing Deviance. A Study of News Organization*. Toronto: University of Toronto Press.

———. 1989. *Negotiating Control: A Study of News Sources*. Toronto: University of Toronto Press.

———. 1991. *Representing Order: Crime, Law and Justice in the News Media*. Toronto: University of Toronto Press.

Erikson, Kai. 1966. *Wayward Puritans: A Study in the Sociology of Deviance*. New York: Wiley.

Esteva, Gustavo. 1994. "Basta! Mexican Indians Say 'Enough.'" *The Ecologist* 24: 85–95.

Farrell, Ronald A., and Carole Case. 1995. *The Black Book and the Mob: The Untold Story of the Control of Nevada's Casinos*. Madison: University of Wisconsin Press.

Felshin, Nina. "Afterword: Women and Children First—Terrorism on the Home Front." Pp. 258–270 in *Violent Persuasions: The Politics and Imagery of Terrorism*, edited by David Brown and Robert Morale. Seattle: Bay Press.

Ferrarotti, Franco. 1980. *L'ipnosi della Violenza*. Milan: Rizzoli.

———. 1995. "Foreshadowings of Postmodernism: Counter-Cultures of the Apocalypse," *International Journal of Politics, Culture and Society* 9(2): 36–88.

Forgacs, David. 1986. "Why Rethink Italian Fascism?" Pp. 1–10 in *Rethinking Italian Fascism*, edited by David Forgacs. London: Lawrence and Wisehart.

Foucault, Michel. 1972. *The Archeology of Knowledge*, translated by A.M. Smith. New York: Harper and Row.

———. (1977) 1979. *Discipline and Punish: The Birth of the Prison*. New York: Vintage Books.

Franchetti, Leopoldo, and Sidney Sonnino. [1876] 1974. "Condizioni Politiche e Amministrative della Sicilia," *Inchiesta in Sicilia, Vol. 1*. Firenze: Vallecchi.

Frank, Andre Gunder. 1993. "Bronze Age World-System Cycles." *Current Anthropology* 34: 383–429.

———, and Barry K. Gills. 1993. *The World System: Five Hundred Years or Five Thousand?* New York: Routledge.

Frye, Northrop. 1957. *Anatomy of Criticism*. Princeton: Princeton University Press.

Galli, Giorgio. 1974. *Storia della Societa Italiana dall'Unita a Oggi*. Turin: UTET.

Geertz, Clifford. 1981. *Negara: The Theater State in Nineteenth Century Bali*. Princeton: Princeton University Press.

Gibbs, Jack. 1989. "Conceptualization of Terrorism." *American Sociological Review* 54 (June): 329–340.

Girard, Rene. 1977. *Violence and the Sacred*. Baltimore: Johns Hopkins University Press.

Goldaber, Irving. 1979. "A Typology of Hostage-Takers." *The Police Chief*: 21–23.

Goldberg, David Theo. 1993. *Racist Culture*. Cambridge: Basil Blackwell.

———, ed. 1994. *Multiculturalism: A Critical Reader*. Cambridge: Blackwell Publishers.

Goldschlager, Alain. 1985. "On Ideological Discourse," *Semiotica* 54: 165–176.

Goode, Erich, and Nachman Ben-Yehuda. 1994. *Moral Panics: The Social Construction of Deviance*. Cambridge: Blackwell.

Gramsci, Antonio. 1966. *Quaderni Del Carcere: Letteratura e Vita Nazionale*. Giulio Einaudi Editore.

———. 1971. *Selections from the Prison Notebooks*. New York: International Publishers.

Grundle, Stephen, and Simon Parker. 1996. *The New Italian Republic*. New York: Routledge.

Gurr, Ted R. 1980. *Handbook of Political Conflict: Theory and Research*. New York: The Free Press.

Gusfield, Joseph. 1976. "The Literary Rhetoric of Science: Comedy and Pathos in Drinking Driver Research." *American Sociological Review* 41 (February): 16–34.

Hacker, F. 1976. *Crusaders,Criminals, Crazies: Terrorists and Terrorism in Our Time*. New York: W.W. Norton.

Handler, Jeffrey. 1990. "Socioeconomic Profile of an American Terrorist: 1960s and 1970s." *Terrorism* 13: 195–213.

Heidegger, Martin. 1971. *Poetry, Language, Thought*. New York: Harper and Row.

Hegel, G.W.F. (1837) 1970. *Vorlesungen über die Philosophie der Geschichte* [Readings about the Philosophy of History]. Frankfurt am Main.

Held, David. 1989. *Political Theory and the Modern State*. Stanford: Stanford University Press.

Herberg, Will. 1955. *Protestant, Catholic, Jew: An Essay in American Religious Sociology*. New York: Doubleday.

Hobsbawm, Eric. 1969. *Bandits*. New York: Pantheon Books.

Hofmann, Paul. 1990. *That Fine Italian Hand*. New York: Henry Holt and Co.

Hofstadter, Albert. 1955. "The Scientific and Literary Uses of Language." Pp. 291–335 in *Symbols and Society*, edited by Lyman Bryson, Louis Finkelstein, Hudson Hoagland, and R. MacIver. New York: Conference on Science, Philosophy and Religion and Their Relation to the Democratic Way of Life, Inc.

Huggins, Martha. 1987. "U.S.-Supported State Terror: A History of Police Training in Latin America." *Crime and Social Justice* 27–28: 149–171.

Hugo, Pierre. 1988. "Towards Darkness and Death: Racial Demonology in South Africa." *The Journal of Modern African Studies* 26 (4): 567–590.

Inverarity, James M., Lauderdale, Pat, and Barry C. Feld. 1983. *Law and Society*. Boston: Little Brown and Co.

Jameson, Fredric. 1983. *The Political Unconscious: Narrative as a Socially Symbolic Act*. Ithaca: Cornell University Press.

Jenkins, Brian. 1979. "The Terrorist Mindset and Terrorist Decision-making: Two Areas of Ignorance." Santa Monica: The Rand Corporation.

———. 1985. *The Future Course of International Terrorism*. Santa Monica: Rand.

Kirby, Andrew. 1993. *Power/Resistance*. Bloomington: Indiana University Press.

Kressel, Neil J. 1996. *Mass Hate: The Global Rise of Genocide and Terror*. New York: Plenum.

Kuhn, Thomas. 1979. *The Structure of Scientific Revolutions*. Chicago: University of Chicago Press.

Lacan, Jacques. 1966. *Écrits*. Paris: Editions du Seuil.

Lang, Amy S. 1981. "Antinomianism and the 'Americanization' of Doctrine." *New England Quarterly* 54: 225–242.

LaPalombara, Joseph. 1965. "Italy: Fragmentation, Isolation and Alienation." Pp. 282–329 in *Political Culture and Political Development*, edited by Lucian Pye and Sydney Verba. Princeton: Princeton University Press.

Laqueur, Walter. 1986. "Reflections on Terrorism," *Foreign Affairs* 65(1): 86–89.

Larson, J.F. 1986. "Television and U.S. Foreign Policy: The Case of the Iran Hostage Crisis." *Journal of Communication* 36(4): 108–130.

Lasch, Christopher. 1979. *The Culture of Narcissism*. New York: W.W. Norton and Co.

Lauderdale, Pat, and James Inverarity. 1980. "From Apolitical to Political Analyses of Deviance." Pp. 15–44 in *A Political Analysis of Deviance* edited by Pat Lauderdale. Minneapolis: University of Minnesota Press.

Lauderdale, Pat. 1980. *A Political Analysis of Deviance*. Minneapolis: University of Minnesota Press.

———, Steve McLaughlin, and Annamarie Oliverio. 1990. "Levels of Analysis, Theoretical Orientations and Degrees of Abstraction." *The American Sociologist* 21(1): 29–40.

———, and Michael Cruit. 1993. *The Struggle for Control: A Study of Law, Disputes and Deviance.* Albany: SUNY Press.

———, and Annamarie Oliverio. 1995. "Justice Ethics and Liberation." *International Journal of Comparative Sociology* 36: 131–148.

———. 1995. "Law and Nature." *Controversen in der Philosophie* 8: 37–55.

Le Carre, John. 1984. *The Little Drummer Girl.* Toronto: Bantam Books.

Lenzi, Mario. 1981. *Il Giornale.* Roma: Editori Riuniti.

Leverenz, David. 1980. *The Language of Puritan Feeling: An Exploration in Literature, Psychology and Social History.* New Brunswick, N.J.: Rutgers University Press.

Liebkind, Karmela. 1979. *The Social Psychology of Minority Identity: A Case Study of Intergroup Identification: Theoretical Refinement and Methodological Experimentation.* Helsinki: University of Helsinki, Dept. of Social Psychology.

"Lost in the Terrorist Theatre." Forum, October 1984. *Harper's.* Pp. 20–25.

Lyttelton, Adrian. 1973. *Italian Fascisms: From Pareto to Gentile.* New York: Harper and Row.

Lumley, Bob, and Philip Schlesinger. 1982. "The Press the State and Its Enemies, the Italian Case." *Sociological Review* 30(4): 603–626.

McCarthy, Patrick. 1995. *The Crisis of the Italian State: From the Origins of the Cold War to the Fall of Berlusconi.* New York: St. Martin's Press.

McLoughlin, William G. 1978. *Revivals, Awakenings and Reform.* Chicago: The University of Chicago Press.

McLuhan, Marshall. 1964. *Understanding Media.* New York: Signet.

Manning, Peter. 1989. "Violence." *National Institute of Justice* 14: 5–21.

Merrell, Floyd. 1985. *A Semiotic Theory of Texts.* New York: Mouton de Gruyter.

Merton, Robert. 1968. *Social Theory and Social Structure.* Third Edition. New York: Free Press.

Miller, Abraham H. 1982. *Terrorism, the Media and the Law.* New York: Transnational Publishers, Inc.

Mills, C. Wright. 1959. *The Sociological Imagination*. New York: Oxford University Press.

Minson, Jeffrey. 1985. *Genealogies of Morals*. London: MacMillan Press.

Mouffe, Chantal. 1979. *Gramsci and Marxist Theory*. Boston: Routledge and Kegan Paul.

Moxon-Brown, Edward. 1994. *European Terrorism*. New York: MacMillan.

Moyers, Bill. 1988. *The Secret Government: The Constitution in Crisis*. Cabin John, Md.: Seven Locks Press.

Munzi, Ulderico, and Roberto Stagno. 1985. "Navi da Guerra Puntano Sull' "Achille Lauro." *Corriere della Sera* (October). Milano.

Namaste, Ki. 1993. "Semiotics and/as Social Theory." *American Journal of Semiotics* 1–2: 177–200.

Nanetti, Raffaella. 1988. *Growth and Territorial Policies: The Italian Model of Social Capitalism*. New York: Pinter Publishers.

Nash, Kate. 1994. "The Feminist Production of Knowledge: Is Deconstruction a Practice for Women." *Feminist Review* 47: 65–77.

Nilsen, Alleen Pace. 1977. "Sexism in English." Pp. 200–208 in *Language*, edited by Virginia Clark. New York: St. Martin's Press.

Oliverio, Annamarie, and Carolyn Desjardins. 1993. "Women's Leadership and Spirituality: A Different Choice." *Fifth International Interdisciplinary Congress on Women Proceedings*. San Jose, Costa Rica.

———, and Pat Lauderdale. 1996. "Therapeutic States and Attention Deficits: Differential Cross-National Diagnostics and Treatments." *International Journal of Politics, Culture and Society* 10(2): 355–373.

O'Neill, M.J. 1986. *Terrorist Spectaculars: Should T.V. Coverage be Curbed?* New York: Priority Press.

Petras, James. 1987. "Political Economy of State Terror: Chile, El Salvador and Brazil." *Crime and Social Justice* 27–28: 88–109.

Pfohl, Stephen. Unpublished Manuscript. *Terror of the Simulacra: Struggles for Justice and the Postmodern*. Presented at Arizona State University, School of Justice Studies, 1987.

Pisano, Vittorfranco S. *The Dynamics of Subversion and Violence in Contemporary Italy.* Stanford: Hoover Institution Press.

Polsky, Andrew. 1991. *The Rise of the Therapeutic State.*

Princeton: Princeton University Press.

Pudaloff, Ross J. 1985. "Sign and Subject: Antinomianism in Massachusetts Bay." *Semiotica* 54 1/2: 147–163.

Ramirez, Francisco O., and John Boli. 1987. "Global Patterns of Educational Institutionalization," and "On the Union of States and Schools." Pp. 150–197 in *Institutional Structure*, edited by George Thomas, John Meyer, Francisco O. Ramirez, and John Boli. Beverly Hills: Sage.

Raum, Tom. 1995. "Clinton Vows 'Aggressive' Stand Against Terrorism." *The Associated Press* (April 24): 1–4.

Reich, Michael R. 1991. *Toxic Politics: Responding to Chemical Disasters.* Ithaca: Cornell University Press.

Reid, Christopher. 1985. *Edmund Burke and the Practice of Political Writing.* New York: Gill and MacMillan.

Renner, Michael. 1993. "Preparing for Peace." Pp. 139–157 in *State of the World*, edited by Linda Starke. New York: W.W. Norton and Co.

Romano, Sergio. 1984. "The Roots of Italian Terrorism." *Policy Review* 25: 25–27.

Rubin, Jeffrey Z. 1986. "Theatre of Terror," *Psychology Today* (March). Washington, D.C.

Russell, Charles A., and Bowman H. Miller. 1977. "Profile of a Terrorist." *Military Review* 58(8): 33.

Said, Edward W. 1988. "Identity, Negation and Violence," *New Left Review* 71: 46–60.

Saphir, E. 1929. "The Status of Linguistics as a Science." *Language* 5: 207–214.

Sassoon, Anne S. 1987. *Gramsci's Politics.* Minneapolis: University of Minnesota Press.

Saussure, Ferdinand de. (1916) 1986. Cours de Linguistique Generale [Course in General Linguistics]. Edited by Charles Bally and Albert Sechehaye and translated by Roy Harris. London: G. Duckworth.

Schmid, Alex P., and Albert J. Jongman. 1988. *Political Terrorism*. New York: North-Holland Publishing Company.

Schulte-Sasse, Jochen. 1987. "Electronic Media and Cultural Politics in the Reagan Era: The Attack on Libya and Hands Across America as Postmodern Events." *Cultural Critique* 8: 123–152.

Schultz, R.H. Jr., and J.M. Schmauder. 1994. "Regional Conflicts and U.S. Interests in the 1990s." *Studies in Conflict and Terrorism* 17: 1–38.

Shank, Gregory. 1987. "Contragate and Counterterrorism: An Overview." *Crime and Social Justice* 27–28: i–xxvii.

Sharif, Idris. 1996. *The Success of Political Terrorist Events*. New York: University Press of America.

Simonson, Lee. 1968. "The Ideas of Adolphe Appia." Pp. 27–50 in *The Theory of the Modern Stage* edited by Eric Bentley. New York: Penguin Books.

Smith, Brent L., and Kathryn D. Morgan. 1994. "Terrorists Right and Left: Empirical Issues in Profiling American Terrorists." *Studies in Conflict and Terrorism* 17: 39–57.

Smith, W.E. 1985. "Terror Aboard Flight 847." *Time*, 125(25) (June 24): 18–26.

Stehr, Nico. 1994. *Knowledge Societies*. Thousand Oaks, Cal.: Sage.

Stevens, Robert W. 1976. *Vain Hopes, Grim Realities: The Economic Consequences of the Vietnam War*. New York: New Viewpoints.

Stohl, Michael. (1983) 1988. *The Politics of Terrorism*. New York: Marcel Dekker, Inc.

Stout, Harry. 1982. "Word and Order in Colonial New England." Pp. 19–38 in *The Bible in America: Essays in Cultural History*, edited by Nathan O. Hatch. New York: Oxford University Press.

Targ, Harry R. 1988. "Societal Structure and Revolutionary Terrorism: A Preliminary Investigation." Pp. 127–152 in *The Politics of Terrorism*, edited by M. Stohl. New York: Marcel Dekker, Inc.

Thomas, George, John W. Meyer, Francisco O. Ramirez, and John Boli. 1987. *Institutional Structure: Constituting State, Society, and the Individual*. Beverly Hills: Sage.

Thornton, R. 1987. *American Indian Holocaust and Survival*. University of Oklahoma Press.

Tilly, Charles. 1985. "War Making and State Making as Organized Crime." Pp. 169–191 in *Bringing the State Back In*, edited by Peter B. Evans, Dietrich Rueschemeyer, and Theda Skocpol. Cambridge: Cambridge University Press.

Tocqueville, Alexis de. [1862] 1968. "Some Observations on the Drama Amongst Democratic Nations." Pp. 479–484 in *The Theory of the Modern Stage*, edited by Eric Bentley, translated by Henry Reeve, and revised by Francis Bowen. Kingsport, Tenn.: Kingsport Press.

Tower, J., Muskie, E., and B. Scowcroft. 1987. *Report of the President's Special Review Board*. Washington, D.C.: New Executive Office Building.

U.S. Congress Senate Committee on Labor and Human Resources. Subcommittee on Children, Family, Drugs and Alcoholism. 1990. *Domestic Violence: Terrorism in the Home*. Washington, D.C.: 1–118.

U.S. Department of State. 1988. "Patterns of Global Terrorism: 1985." Pp. 317–372 in *The Politics of Terrorism*, edited by M. Stohl. New York: Marcel Dekker, Inc.

U.S. National Advisory Committee on Criminal Justice Standards and Goals. 1976. *Disorders and Terrorism: Report of the Task Force on Disorders and Terrorism*. Washington, D.C.: GPO.

Virilio, Paul. 1986. *Speed and Politics*. New York: Semiotext(e).

Wagner-Pacifici, Robin E. 1986. *The Moro Morality Play: Terrorism as Social Drama*. Chicago: University of Chicago Press.

Wallace, Anthony F.C. 1970. *The Death and Rebirth of the Seneca: The History and Culture of the Great Iroquois Nation, Their Destruction and Demoralization and Their Cultural Revival at the Hands of the Indian Visionary, Handsome Lake*. New York: Alfred A. Knopf.

Walzer, Michael. 1977. *Just and Unjust Wars: A Moral Argument with Historical Illustrations*. New York: Basic Books.

Wardlaw, Grant. 1982. *Political Terrorism: Theory, Tactics and Countermeasures*. New York: Cambridge University Press.

von Werlhof, Claudia. 1989. *Transforming Nature Into a Man (into male): The Political Project of Reproductive Technologies*. Paper delivered at the New Orleans Women's Studies Symposium.

Weber, Max. 1954. On Law in Economy and Society. Edited by Max Rheinstein. Cambridge, Mass.: Harvard University Press.

———. 1958. "Politics as a Vocation." Pp. 77–128 in *From Max Weber: Essays in Sociology*, edited and translated by Hans Heinrich Gerth and C. Wright Mills. New York: Oxford University Press.

Wilkinson, Paul. 1986. *Terrorism and the Liberal State*. London: Macmillan.

———. 1990. *Conflict Studies, 236: Terrorist Targets and Tactics: New Risks to World Order*. Washington, D.C.: RISCT and the Center for Security Studies.

Wittgenstein, Ludwig. 1921. "Tractatus Logico-Philosophicus." P. 33 in *Annalende Naturphilosophie*, edited by Ostwalds. German-English edition: London.

White, Hayden. 1973. *Metahistory: The Historical Imagination in Nineteenth Century Europe*. Baltimore: Johns Hopkins Press.

———. 1987. *The Content of the Form: Narrative Discourse and Historical Representation*. Baltimore: The Johns Hopkins University Press.

Whorf, E. L. 1956. *Language Thought and Reality*. New York: Carroll.

Zulaika, Joseba, and William Douglas. 1996. *Terror and Taboo: The Follies Fables and Faces of Terrorism*. New York: Routledge.

INDEX